HOW TO TAPE INSTANT ORAL BIOGRAPHIES

HOW TO TAPE INSTANT ORAL BIOGRAPHIES

Drawings by Tom Bloom
BILL ZIMMERMAN
author of *Make Beliefs*

BETTERWAY BOOKS
CINCINNATI, OH

03 02 01 00 99   5 4 3 2 1

Library of Congress Cataloging-in-Publication Data

Zimmerman, William.
   How to tape instant oral biographies / by Bill Zimmerman.
      p.   cm.
   Some new material has been added since the 1992 ed. Includes index.
   ISBN 1-55870-526-0 (alk. paper)
   1. Oral biography. I. Title.
CT25.Z548   1999
920'.0028—dc21   99-14209
                                    CIP

Production edited by Bob Beckstead
Interior designed by Sandy Kent
Cover/interior illustrations by Tom Bloom
Production coordinated by Erin Boggs

Table of Contents

A New Edition for the New Millennium

The trip you are about to take in reading and using *How to Tape Instant Oral Biographies* is perfect preparation for entering the New Millennium.

One of the most important treasures you can take with you into the next century is your family's history and its stories. For the new years to come, each of us will need durable constants in our life to ground us in the fast-moving future. And such constants will be the collected memories of our family's history, telling us how its members made their individual journeys in the world.

There is much to learn from our ancestors. Their lives, as you will learn from using this book, show us how they made their way, how they overcame hardships and difficulties, and what dreams and hopes they shared (which are not so very different from our own). They can serve as a good example for us as we cross over into the new century. To understand our past is to be better prepared for our future and the futures of generations to come.

When I originally published this book myself 20 years ago, my intent was to bring younger and older generations together to learn from one another through the asking of questions and the listening to answers. The intent has not changed in this new edition. If anything, you will find even more questions to pose to others in the "Questions to Ask" section. And you will also find in this edition new chapters to help the generations review the past and imaginatively explore the future together.

There is, for example, a "Time Capsules for the New Millennium" section in which both those being interviewed for their oral biographies and those doing the interviews can place their hopes, dreams and predictions for the future. Fill them out, date them and open them sometime in the middle of the new century. There is also a special "Make Beliefs Activities" section in which your relatives can write, color or draw their responses to a variety of questions that will provoke their imaginations and help them think more creatively about their lives. This should provide you both with much fun.

In this new edition, too, I have included a "What Is a *Family*?" chapter in recognition of the fact that the way we think of family has changed significantly since the time I first wrote the book. This chapter tries to provide useful interviewing information for families that may be multiracial, multiethnic or multi-religious in composition, for families in which the heads of households are gay, for families headed by single parents or by grandparents, or for families with stepparents and stepchildren. The reality is that today new kinds of families have emerged to join the traditional mom-and-pop ones.

I also have added "A Personal Essay" that talks about what I learned from the experience of taping an instant oral biography with my own mother, and about how both the writing of the book and the tapings changed my life. I hope that the recordings you will make with your own family or friends and loved ones will change your life for the better, too.

Please enjoy this new edition for the New Millennium, and may the new century bring you much happiness and personal growth!

Yours sincerely,

Bill Zimmerman

Bill Zimmerman

PREFACE:

A Sense of Family

Everyone has a story to tell.
If only someone would listen,
If only someone would ask.

A sense of family has always been important in my life. Family has been the source of strength to me, as well as the source of much pain.

Much of my early adult years was spent in breaking away from my people, searching for my dead father, rebelling against family closeness.

I tried to establish a new family made up only of people I had chosen to be its members.

I chose a career in journalism as a way to broaden my life, and found after interviewing hundreds of strangers I was better able to know myself. I learned that many of my fears and my dreams were shared by others.

The years passed. I am now the father of a young daughter, and have reached the same age my parents were when they had young children. I judge them less now. I can appreciate their struggles and understand more clearly why they were the way they were.

I wrote this book—sort of a how-to-do-it

guide for recording one's family history—to help me better understand my parent's lives, and hence my own.

I wrote this book also to help preserve for myself, my daughter and perhaps for generations to come something of the voice of my family that is very special. I wrote it to draw us all closer, and to give each of us a chance to record and appreciate our stories.

—BZ

CHAPTER ONE

What's an Instant Oral Biography?

Grandma, what were you like as a little girl?
Dad, how'd you meet Mom? What was she like then?
Cindy, what was the turning point of your life?
Aunt Ann, what was I like when I was little?

Remember asking the questions? Remember the stories you heard? Wouldn't you give much of what you own today if you could hear the voice or advice of an honored ancestor or special relative who is no longer around?

Every person—not just famous people—has stories, a biography and a family history worth telling and saving. But not everyone knows how to record that history quickly and easily, or in a form that is organized and can be preserved.

Tracking Your Family Chronicles

This book presents a method to help you become an instant biographer or reporter and save the stories of your family and friends. It encourages you to capture the special voices and stories of the people you love and respect while they are still with you and their memories are still sharp.

The *Instant Oral Biographies* concept proposes that, with the use of tape recorders, videotape systems and simple interviewing techniques, *anyone*—child or adult—can easily prepare oral biographies to track their family's chronicles and development much in the same way still cameras and home movies traditionally have been used for this purpose.

Only now, instead of cameras alone, we also can use audiotape and videotape recorders—the tools journalists use to conduct interviews and preserve large amounts of information.

The objective of *Instant Oral Biographies* is to help you create a family library of spoken histories that you and future generations can listen to, both to understand the people in your families better and to help you answer some of the questions you have about your background.

Such recordings, in helping us learn more about our families and our friends, also enable us to learn more about ourselves. These are the people who influenced our lives and caused us, in part at least, to be the way we are.

Becoming an "Instant Reporter"

The guides in this book apply interviewing techniques I have learned and developed over the past 20 years as a professional journalist. I have interviewed thousands of people for their stories—from the chief executives of the world's largest banks to people in the street looking for work.

These guides incorporate teaching techniques I have used as an editor of daily newspapers to train numerous inexperienced people to become, in time, outstanding journalists in their fields.

This book presents instructions to teach you how to interview relatives and friends; a comprehensive list of suggested questions to ask in recording family biographies; and family history sheets that you can fill in as you interview or later on. The sheets have been duplicated to allow at least two people in a family to fill them in.

You are encouraged to add your own questions; space has been provided to write those questions down or to make notes on what you learn during the interview.

The section on suggested questions was designed to answer what is perhaps the most difficult problem any interviewer faces—sustaining a conversation with someone by asking readily understood, provocative questions that elicit meaningful and interesting answers.

The questions in this book include both straightforward ones to get short, factual responses in some chronological order—important to any biography—and more open-ended questions to encourage people to open up and give broader responses.

Interviewing Yourself

I also believe that with the use of the suggested questions anyone can interview herself and make an autobiographical tape.

A parent, for example, could make a recording to send to his child on a special occasion, such as a birthday or an anniversary.

Similarly, oral biographies can provide you with a means to hand down to your family and friends special messages, advice or testaments that complement the written letters and legacies you wish to leave to others.

Taping one's own history could also be a very beneficial experience for, say, a relative who is often alone or bedridden and would like to take on a useful activity.

Oral histories also provide the visually impaired with an easy method to record their stories.

In putting together these oral biography guidelines, I hold the basic premise that there is value in all people—that each of us has something to say that is worth telling others and worth remembering.

More of us would believe this if we could be encouraged to talk more and answer questions such as the ones posed in this book.

There is no doubt we enjoy sitting together and trading memories with one another; most of us like to hear about other peoples' lives to see how they coped with the basic life processes—making a living, raising a family and finding the strength to overcome personal crises.

We all like to compare notes.

The oral interviewing techniques I am proposing here will give everyone a chance to tell his story with help from you as the interested family member or friend, the "instant reporter."

Think of the wonderful possibilities of putting together such oral biographies:

- They provide a means by which a family can be drawn together in a more meaningful way to record and listen to the stories of grandparents, parents, aunts, uncles and children. What better way for a grandchild to learn the stories of a grandparent and appreciate the special richness of our distinct backgrounds?
- They enhance the happiness and poignancy of our meetings, especially such family occasions as a parent's birthday, an anniversary, Mother's Day, Father's Day or Grandparents' Day, religious holidays and vacations.
- They make people feel better about themselves. Richness is given by those telling the stories of their lives *and* by those who ask, and thus give others the chance to share— and save—their histories.
- They preserve our special voices at a time when the world and its values are changing so rapidly, and when individual family members are scattering around the earth.
- They help us in our quest to reach back and trace our history, and support our belief that our traditions are worth preserving.
- Oral biographies help elderly people break their silences by making them feel they are being heard. They can be used by those who work with the aged to help them capture the stories and advice they want to leave to family and friends.
- The interviews for oral biographies can be

used in schools and colleges to develop students' listening and verbal skills and their understanding of history. The guides here can help them ask questions and recall answers, and can teach them something of the process of journalism and historical research.

The interviews can help young people realize, as journalists do, that there is much to learn from other people, and that we each have a history that has value. Students should be encouraged to listen to one another's tapes in order to share their heritages.

- The interviews can be used by specialists who provide social, religious, health, educational and counseling services as a way to draw people out of their problems.
- The interview techniques suggested here can also be applied by all of us in our daily lives to gain information and make our interactions with others, including strangers, easier and more meaningful.

They also can be employed at times of mourning when people gather together to capture memories of the people we loved. Taping the stories about a person can be a way to deal with grief.

The Satisfaction of Sharing

There also are unexpected benefits in making oral biographies. In my own case, after making a biographical tape of my mother, I'm still not sure which one of us got more satisfaction and good feeling from the experience, she or I.

She felt better for having shared some of her life with me. She said she had wanted to say some of the things we discussed long before the taping, but had not had the occasion to do so.

The interviewing, she said, gave her a certain emotional release that she felt positive about, and it gave us both a constructive way to explore the past together in order to come to closer terms with one another.

I felt better for having a deeper understanding of why certain things were the way they were.

I listen to the tapes from time to time, and I am proud to have them and to be able to share them with my wife and daughter.

My mother is dead now, but I will always be able to hear her voice.

Three generations together—author's wife, Teodorina Bello de Zimmerman, with daughter, Carlota, and Pastora Arena Garcia.

CHAPTER TWO

How to Interview People

Don't be intimidated by the thought of doing an *interview*. Just keep these simple things in mind:

1 *An interview is a way for you to talk with someone, with the help of questions, for the purpose of obtaining information about that person's life.*

In making an *Instant Oral Biography*, you are trying to record parts of someone's life story.

Keep in mind what all journalists think about when they are asking questions—every fact has several parts to it that answer the questions who? what? where? when? why? and how?

2 *The best interviews occur when both the interviewer and the person being questioned have had time to prepare a little and think about what they want to accomplish through the interview.*

Before you actually begin an interview it is important that you explain what your purpose is in compiling this oral biography.

You might say, for example:

"Mama, I'd like to hear your story, what your parents were like, what your earliest memories are and what life was like when you grew up. I'd like you to tell me and my children what your beliefs are. I will be using the tape recorder when you speak to make a living record of you, as well as other members of our family, a record that we can have for always and that future generations can hear."

As you say this, in fact, you might even want to test the recorder, tape what you are saying and then play it back to the person being interviewed. It's a way to begin and to show the other person how the recording process takes place. It can also help to overcome the fear of making the tapes.

Also, when calling your relatives or friends to make an appointment for an interview, ask them to gather some old pictures of their parents and family members, as well as documents such as passports, citizenship papers, marriage and birth certificates you can review together. Old diaries, letters, postcards, scrapbooks and newspaper clippings can be helpful, too.

Looking at old pictures with someone can often help people remember stories or experiences that will be wonderful to have as part of the oral biography. Read letters aloud. Listen to favorite music together.

You might even want to bring an atlas with you to see where your relatives lived before they came to this country. A paperback, such as the Rand McNally *Historical Atlas of the World,* is an excellent tool to trace some of the older countries that have been absorbed by larger nations.

3 *Try to overcome your own fears of handling a tape recorder, which will be playing all the while you are interviewing.*

The machine should be looked upon as an aid, a friend if you will, just as it is the companion of thousands of journalists.

So before you begin interviewing, try it out, practice with it, fool around with it and make mistakes with it. You will see that, with practice, it works *for* you, not against you. It is much easier to record than to just write answers down. (You can do both.)

If you don't own a tape recorder, you can rent one. Look in the phone directory under the subject listing "Recorders, Sound—Equipment & Supplies."

Bring extra batteries to the interview, if you use them for your recorder, and extra tapes. Make sure the tapes are of the best quality available because you want them to last for many, many years.

Also take a pen or pencil with you in case you want to make some notes to yourself as you go along in the interview. You can use the special pages set aside in this book. Note taking reinforces listening.

4 *Think of an interview as having a conversation in which you are asking most of the questions to keep the talk going and to keep it interesting.*

To have a good talk, try to conduct the interview in a quiet place where there are just the two of you so that some intimacy is achieved and thoughtful answers can be obtained.

You might want to do the interview in a kitchen or living room in which both of you are seated comfortably. Have a cup of coffee or tea together as you talk.

Later, as the interviewing process progresses, it's possible that you might want to have other family members or friends join in and add to the responses.

5 *Try to reassure the person being interviewed.*

Some peoples' initial reactions to a request to do an oral biography might be to say that they have nothing important to tell you. But you know better. It is important you get across the message that you believe what they have to say has value.

Try to convey to them that their answers and thoughts are important: They will be part of a family's record of its history and its survival, and you are trying to preserve their voice.

When people tell you, "I have nothing important to say," they really are saying, "Encourage me. Help me see my life has meaning."

6 *At first the people you interview may be somewhat nervous or apprehensive. This should not be surprising, because most people have never been interviewed before.*

You might even find, as I have, that until the people you interview get comfortable they will tend to lead the conversation where they want it to go, and perhaps will not give you the types of responses you want.

But don't worry about letting people wander a little in giving their answers: That's how you get interesting information. Just make a note about what point you want to go back to, and return to it later.

Don't feel you have to be in total control over the interview all the time. It takes away the fun. The best interviewers regain control in a quiet way by coming back later to the questions that interest them.

7 *The most effective interviewers also give as much as they take.*

This means they listen as carefully as possible to what a person is saying—or *not* saying.

Listening well is important: If you hear an answer that is interesting, you can be ready to encourage the person to elaborate further. It is important to convey to the person you are interviewing that you really want to hear their point of view.

I have found from my own experience in asking questions that people often don't come right out with clear answers. They may offer cues or phrases instead, or start a sentence they don't finish. Listen carefully, because this may be someone's way of signaling you to ask them more about what they meant to say.

8 *A good interviewer brings out the best in her subject and is often a prompter of inner thoughts.*

You might offer an example from your own experience to help someone being interviewed better understand the question you are asking.

Or you might help them recall an answer by starting the question with a story you remember, such as:

"Remember, Dad, the time we went fishing with Uncle Ed and he fell into the water and . . ."

Help the other person remember, but be patient while they think through what you are asking. You have all the time in the world.

9 *The interview you are conducting is to get the other person's story, not yours, even though the other person may tell you a lot about yourself.*

You may very well know the answers to some of the questions you ask, but for the purpose of compiling an oral record, you should let the person you are interviewing give the answers. And never cut them off.

10 *Let me reassure you about asking questions.*

Despite what your parents or your teachers may have told you when you were little, you shouldn't be afraid to ask people questions.

I agree that it takes some courage and confidence to interview others; I, too, have felt fear and trepidation before interviewing strangers.

But you will be interviewing family and friends. The worst thing that can happen to you is that they will not want to answer a question or will laugh at you. But this is no big deal.

As all journalists do, catch your breath and go on; you always can go back to a question later if you do not initially get a completely satisfactory answer.

Remember, most interviewers ask the same questions many times during an interview until they get an answer they want. They just phrase the question differently each time they ask it.

Most times, however, people will try their best to answer your questions if you show you really are interested—and they will give you wonderful responses.

11 *In reviewing the suggested interview questions in this book, feel free to use only those that interest you the most.*

Change them, or add other questions that you want answers to; and, of course, improvise as you go along in the interview. If you are not asking questions you truly are interested in, it is not likely you will get the effective responses you want to have for the recording.

Also, choose only those questions you feel comfortable with. There were some questions, for example, that I could not bring myself to ask my mother when were making our tape. You can always come back another time with new questions.

12 *Study the questions so that you are familiar with them. You might even want to practice saying them out loud in a quiet corner in your home so that you get used to them.*

You may also want to set particular goals beforehand as to what you hope to come away with from the interview. For instance, you might want to learn more about what you were like as a five-year-old and what was occurring in other family members' lives at that particular point in time; or you might want to gain new insight into a family problem that troubled you.

You may want to focus on finding out what life was like for that person when they were your age. What changes did each decade of growth bring?

You can show the subject the questions in this book before the interview to help them prepare their thoughts, but you do risk losing spontaneity of response.

13 *By no means do you have to ask all the questions you have at one sitting.*

Interviewing can tire both you and the other person. You want to take pleasure in the process; I suggest you do interviews of half-hour to one-hour duration over a number of sessions.

Having several (or many) interviews can do much to make visits with relatives—particularly with parents and grandparents—more meaningful. There then is something to be learned from each visit. And fun to be had, too!

14 *You are asking people to recount their life stories: Remember that recalling different memories will arouse all kinds of feelings and emotions in both you and the person being interviewed—tears, laughter, anger, joy and sadness can come. Respect these emotions; be understanding of the other person's feelings. Be gentle with them.*

Do not worry about pauses, broken sentences, stuttering or any other verbal imperfections that are captured on the tape. After all, these reflect the way we speak and communicate—they are real—and my feeling is we should not edit them out.

Tears may come, too. During her recording my mother cried when she recalled something about her own mother which had touched her. We stopped for a moment, the tape still running, and then went on. She said later that she was glad to have remembered the event, for even with the pain, it helped her remember how she was as a little girl. For me, as I relisten to the recording, that moment of feeling is very precious.

15 *After you finish conducting the interview, reassure the person that what they said was important to you.*

In answering your questions, people are giving you a part of themselves, and they may feel somewhat vulnerable after the experience. Interviewing can be a draining experience for both the person being interviewed and the person asking the questions.

You might want to call the person you interviewed the next day to thank them for helping you learn so much more about the person in your family and for the pleasure it gave you.

16 *Keep yourself as organized as possible, particularly when you are doing a series of interviews that will use many tapes.*

Number each tape on its surface label; note what side of the tape it is; who was being interviewed; who was interviewing; the relationship between the two, such as mother and son; the date; and whether the interviewing was done on a special occasion, such as a birthday.

In fact, it is useful to start each tape with an introduction summarizing this information. You might say, for example: "This is side two of the interview with my mother, Mary Jones, done on May 3, 1999. It is her fiftieth birthday. This is Bill Jones speaking."

If you do another interview with the same person at a later date, you might state at the beginning of the tape that this interview is a continuation of an earlier one done on May 3, 1999.

If a tape runs out right in the middle of someone answering a question, make a written note of where you were at so that when you change the tape you can add a sentence in the beginning to aid in the transition from one tape to another. You might say, for example: "Mother, you were just talking about the time you took that trip to Europe. Please go on."

And to help you keep track of the content of each tape, consider attaching a summary sheet of the subjects covered and where they can be found on the tape. Most tape recorders have a built-in counter for tracking tape footage. (As an example, your summary might note: Mother's first love, 10–85.)

I further suggest you interview people one at a time rather than in groups, which are hard to control and frequently the noise level gets so high it is hard to keep track of who is saying what.

If you decide to interview during one of those rare occasions when people come from far away to gather at one place, such as a wedding, consider drawing people away, one at a time, to a quiet room for a short interview.

Also consider focusing the interviews on one theme or subject, such as their remembrances of the bride or groom when they were children, how they themselves felt on the day of their marriage, or what advice they can offer the newlyweds.

Remember, the more you interview, the better a reporter you will become. The art of being a good interviewer is thinking about what you want to accomplish, asking clear questions, listening carefully and encouraging people to be confident that you respect what they have to say.

CHAPTER THREE

Ideas for Video Oral Biographies

What better use for a new video system than to make a videotape of your favorite people as you interview them about their lives, their memories and their traditions?

Where audiotapes, like radio, provide a certain mystery by making us imagine what people look like behind the voices we hear, video cameras perform the miracle of bringing the people's actual images to us.

Whether you decide to use video for all of or portions of these interviews, here are some ideas for using this medium:

Showing and Telling

From time to time in the interview, take pictures of the old family photographs, documents, maps, newspaper clippings or heirlooms the person refers to. Encourage people to bring their favorite family treasures with them, those collected over the years or those handed down from generation to generation. You can zoom in on the photos as the person talks about them, or even shoot them from behind the shoulder of the person holding them.

A woman being interviewed might want to show a traditional folk costume worn on special national holidays, or even a wedding dress or shawl that was given to her by her mother.

If a family Bible has been kept through the years and important events have been noted in it, why not have the person hold open its pages for you to videotape?

Similarly, a person may want to show a brooch or a pair of earrings, or a favorite piece of china or a glass figurine that was given to her by someone special or on a special occasion.

Think about capturing a picture of the person near a special symbol that characterizes the family name or history. This might be a coat of arms, a book, a religious symbol such as a cross or a mezuzah, or it could be a scarred old table, a porch swing, a cluttered attic or a grown tree planted when you were very young.

You might also want to videotape objects associated with the person you are interviewing. These might be a cluttered desk, a typewriter, a knitting bag or a sewing box, a fishing rod or a model ship.

How about a music stand or an instrument, an old record, a loved pot, a favorite plant, a homemade doll or an easel? In your videotape you may want to show the person handling or using such objects.

Although you are most interested in focusing on the person's entire face, at times you may want to zoom in on the eyes or mouth. At other times you may want to show, with the help of proper lighting, only a silhouette. If the person talks a lot of using his hands, why not focus on them? If he talks about his marriage, why not zoom in on his wedding band?

You may also want to seat a child next to the person you interview to show two generations reaching out to one another. A child often helps draw out people's thoughts and feelings, and can conduct the interview while you tape them both.

Or, if the subject is seated in a favorite room, why not pan the camera around the room as she talks about her life?

Idea-Generators for Video Biographies

Here are other ideas for video: showing someone teaching how to cook or bake a family recipe, singing, making repairs, lighting candles for a holiday, telling stories to children while putting them to bed, reading a favorite poem or passage from a book, dancing, or even showing people listening to the exchange of marriage vows at a wedding or repeating those vows at an anniversary party.

You might also want to film the person playing a record of a loved piece of music or poem and have them talk about the memories it evokes or the meaning it holds in their life. Have them read an old letter aloud.

It is left to you to decide if you, the inter-

viewer, are to be on camera, too, while doing the questioning.

Video Tips

If so, a tripod can be used to position the camera and keep it stationary. If you don't have a tripod, use books to keep the camera stationary. Better yet, why not have another family member or close friend act as cameraperson while you and your subject are engaged in the interview?

Sometimes the reactions of the interviewer to the stories being told can be as interesting and arresting as the face of the person speaking. This is especially true in an interview where a son or daughter learns something new from questioning a parent.

If someone talks about her brother, you may want to focus on a photograph of that person, or later film a short interview with the brother that could be edited into the tape to follow the first mention of him.

It also might be appropriate at the next family gathering to pan the camera across the faces, one by one, of the people mentioned by your subject in her stories. And as you film them, identify them by name. This is particularly important if you are taping a reunion where many people gather. In reviewing an audiotape or videotape, you might decide later to go out and film the places mentioned during the interview. For example, if someone tells you that he first lived in a small cold-water flat when he came to this country, or on a small farm in another country, you may at some point want to visit the site and capture that location on tape.

I would encourage you to have the subject come with you when you do the filming of these places so that he can convey to you first hand the feelings and impressions this reunion brings. The biography then takes on the character of an odyssey, one which each of us takes with our life.

If, however, you cannot physically go to a faraway location, consider having someone who lives there send you a photograph of the place that you can later put on the tape.

Other Important Tips

A final reminder: Before you begin, show the subject how the equipment works as you test it so that he will not be afraid.

Also, because you are making a videotape in which visual image is so important, it is not necessary to use sound throughout or to have the subject talking constantly. Silent moments can add poignancy, drama and emotional depth to a tape as you show the subject simply sitting alone, or perhaps playing with her grandchildren.

As with the oral biographies captured on audiotape, do not forget to record an introduction for each videocassette you use. This should include the subject's name, relation to you, your name, the date, the location and the occasion. This can be spoken by you, or printed on cards that can be videotaped.

You can have fun writing or drawing such introductions, such as coming up with a title like this:

TOUHY FAMILY PRODUCTIONS

PRESENTS

THE VIDEO BIOGRAPHY OF

GRANDMA CELIA EPSTEIN

And how about using the family cat or dog (or iguana) as the mascot for your home production?

If you like, you can involve other family members in producing the video biography: One person does the interviewing, another monitors sound, and another introduces the list of credits at the beginning of the tape and tells who did what. Not a bad way to draw a family closer.

By having other family members participate, you give them the opportunity to become familiar with your equipment, to have fun and, most important, to make grandmother feel that everyone truly wants to know her life stories.

How can you lose?

These suggestions for videotaping *Instant Oral Biographies* are offered with the intention of awakening your own ideas.

Taping an *Instant Biography*—whether on audiotape or videocassette—is a personal adventure between you and your subject. Approach your mission with a sense of care, sensitivity and art. You are creating something beautiful, something eternal.

CHAPTER FOUR

Before You Begin . . .

Before beginning your interview, I suggest you do these things.

- Look over the questions in the next chapter several times, even a day or two before the interview; select and mark off the ones you like, and change the ones you don't like. They are merely a tool to help you get started, and space has been left between questions for you to change them or add your own; there also are work pages at the end of the section to add even others.
- Test your equipment and tape an introduction to the interview. You might begin this way:

    "This is (state your name) speaking. Today (give month, date, year), I am interviewing (state full name of the person) who is my (give the person's relationship to you)."

If the interview is occurring on a special occasion, such as a birthday, say what the occasion is.

- Review the blank family history sheets in this book. As you conduct the interview—or even later on after it is over—you might

want to fill in the names of different people who were mentioned during the interview on the appropriate charts. The family charts have been duplicated to allow each marriage partner to have a set.

- Finally, consider making duplicates of the tapes for your family.

With these duplicates, we can give one another tapes of our life stories and memories in the same way we send letters and cards. We can offer them as presents at reunions.

Storing Tapes

Always buy the best-quality tapes and enclose them in a storage container where they will be protected from dust or extremes of temperature. These tapes should be cared for with love because they are delicate and carry a treasure that you want to preserve. As an extra precaution, if you have the time and patience, consider transcribing them.

People sometimes tell me that they gave their parents a tape recorder for Christmas to record their memories, but that no tapes were ever made. I tell them what their parents really want is to have someone sit down with them and coax the memories out of them; they want interaction.

Now, with recorder, tapes and pen in hand, let's begin. On to the questions.

(And don't forget to turn on the recorder—with a tape inside!)

CHAPTER FIVE

Questions to Ask

Here is a selection of questions to pose to your interview subject. If you think of more, jot them down in the space provided in Chapter 6. You can use the lines separating each question to take notes.

What is your full name? (In interviewing a married woman, ask for her maiden name as well.)

_____

_____

_____

How was your name chosen?

_____

_____

_____

Do you know what your first name means or whom you were named after?

_____

_____

_____

Did you know this person, and what were they like?

_____

_____

_____

Does your family name have a special meaning?

_____

_____

_____

When were you born?

_____

_____

_____

Where—at home, in a hospital, elsewhere? And in what city and country?

_____

_____

_____

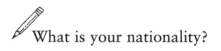 What is your nationality?

_____

_____

_____

Was your family name changed when your family originally came to this country? What was it? In what language?

_____

_____

_____

Who were the first family members to settle in this country? What were their names?

_____

_____

_____

What brought them here, and how did they get the money to come here?

_____

_____

_____

Where did they first arrive? What possessions did they bring with them?

_____

_____

_____

_____

What language did they speak and where exactly did they come from? Did the place they came from have a different name from what it is called today?

_____

_____

_____

Do you know any stories they might have told about what life was like for them before they came here?

_____

_____

_____

Where did they first settle when they came here? How did they make their living?

_____

_____

_____

Do you know when and where your grandparents were born? Their full names?

_____

_____

_____

Do you remember any of the stories your grandparents told you about where they came from or what life was like for them when they were younger? What are some of these stories?

_____

_____

_____

_____

_____

Do you know where they are buried?

_____

_____

_____

What were the full names of your own parents?

_____

_____

_____

When and where were they born and brought up?

_____

_____

What were your parents like?

_____

_____

_____

_____

How did they make a living?

_____

_____

_____

Did you have aunts or uncles? What were their names and what do you remember about them?

_____

_____

_____

Who were your favorite relatives, and why?

_____

_____

_____

_____

_____

Did you have any brothers or sisters? What were their names, and when were they born in relation to you?

_____

_____

_____

_____

What were they like as young people? Do you remember any special or funny stories about them?

_____

_____

_____

_____

Where did you live as a child, and what was your hometown like back then? Can you describe your home for me? What do you miss most about it?

_____

_____

_____

_____

Can you tell me what life was like when you were very young and growing up? What are some of your earliest memories?

_____

_____

_____

_____

What did you look like? What were you like as a young child? Serious? Always getting into trouble? Quiet? Sad? Happy? Can you think of any stories to show the way you were? Any funny ones?

_____

_____

_____

_____

Did you have a nickname? How did you get it?

_____

_____

_____

_____

How much schooling did you have? What was your favorite subject? What subject did you hate?

_____

_____

_____

_____

Did you have a favorite teacher and what was he or she like? How did that teacher influence you?

_____

_____

_____

_____

_____

Did you work as a child? What did you do?

_____

_____

_____

_____

What did you like doing most as a child? What games or instruments did you play? Did you have a favorite pet or toy?

_____

_____

_____

_____

Who were your best friends and what did you do together?

_____

_____

_____

_____

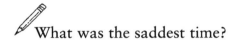 What is the happiest memory in your childhood and when did it happen?

_____

_____

_____

_____

What was the saddest time?

_____

_____

_____

_____

What was your first experience with death? What happened? What did it mean to you? How did you deal with the loss?

_____

_____

_____

_____

_____

What beliefs or ideas do you think your parents tried to teach you?

_____

_____

_____

_____

_____

Who do you think influenced your life the most when you were young, and in what way?

_____

_____

_____

_____

_____

What great person have you known in your life? What made them special?

_____

_____

_____

_____

_____

What were your teenage years like?

_____

_____

_____

_____

_____

What goals and ambitions did you have as a young person, and what goals, if any, did your family have for you?

_____

_____

_____

_____

_____

Did you go to college? What did you study?

_____

_____

_____

What led you to choose the type of work you do or did? What is there about it you liked the most? The least?

_____

_____

_____

_____

When did you start working, and what kinds of jobs were your first ones? What were they like, and how did you do on them?

_____

_____

_____

How much money did you make?

_____

_____

_____

Who was the first president you voted for?

_____

_____

_____

When did you first meet your (husband, wife, partner)? Under what circumstances?

_____

_____

_____

_____

_____

What was (he, she) like when you first met? What attracted you to (him, her)? Or did you dislike one another at first? Why?

_____

_____

_____

How old were you both?

_____

_____

_____

What was your courting like?

_____

_____

How soon after meeting did you marry?

_____

_____

_____

_____

What was life like in the early days of your marriage?

_____

_____

_____

_____

Where did you live? Was it hard to get by? How did you make your living? What was a typical day like for you at work or home?

_____

_____

_____

_____

Did you have any problems in the early years of your marriage? What about? What advice do you offer others for living together?

_____

_____

_____

_____

_____

Did you go to war? Which one? Where were you stationed and what was it like? How long did you serve and in what branch?

_____

_____

_____

_____

_____

When did you have children? (Ask for names of the children, the date each was born and the place.) What were your and your spouse's feelings during the pregnancy? What dreams did you have? Did anything unusual happen at birth?

_____

_____

_____

_____

_____

Who was each child named after? (If children were adopted or came from other marriages, ask about the events surrounding these events.)

_____

_____

_____

_____

What were the children like? How did they differ from one another?

_____

_____

_____

When you think back to the children when they were very young, what stories come to mind about them? How did the children change your life?

_____

_____

_____

_____

How do you raise children to be good human beings?

_____

_____

_____

_____

What do you remember about me as a child? What was I like then? Whom do I take after? Was I very different from the way I am today?

_____

_____

_____

_____

What values did you try to impart to the children—religious, moral, social, other?

_____

_____

_____

_____

If a marriage partner has died, ask about when this occurred and how. Where are they buried?

_____

_____

_____

_____

If a divorce or separation occurred, ask about when this happened and the events that led to it. If there were other marriages, you might want to ask the person being interviewed about them—to whom were they married, when and where did the marriage occur, how did they meet and what children came from the union?

_____

_____

_____

_____

Looking back, what do you think has been the happiest time in your life? What was the worst? How do you get over sad periods? What helps you attain peace of spirit?

_____

_____

_____

_____

What do you think was the turning point in your life? How did your life change after this event? How did you learn to stand on your own two feet? When?

_____

_____

_____

_____

_____

What have been the major accomplishments in your life?

_____

_____

_____

_____

What have been the biggest problems, mistakes or adversities in your life? How did you overcome them, or what did you learn from them? How did they affect your life?

_____

_____

_____

_____

If you were to give advice to me or my children today or even to the children to come in our family's future generations, what would it be? What have you learned from life? What has been its biggest surprise?

_____

_____

_____

_____

What do you think is the best way to conduct our lives?

_____

_____

_____

What do you think your strengths are? What special things do you know that you are proud of?

_____

_____

_____

_____

What are your deepest values?

_____

_____

_____

_____

What makes you happy?

_____

_____

_____

_____

What makes you sad?

_____

_____

_____

_____

How do you overcome your fears?

_____

_____

_____

_____

✏ What activities do you enjoy most—sports, cooking, reading, working, music, studying a certain subject, traveling? Others?

_____

_____

_____

_____

✏ What is the most wonderful place you visited? What is your favorite time of year or holiday?

_____

_____

_____

_____

✏ Is there a particular thought, or a saying, or a joke, or a poem or a song you would like to tell, read, recite or sing for me? I would love to hear it.

_____

_____

_____

_____

_____

Is there a story that was told to you as a child that you would like to recall for me? What is it?

_____

_____

_____

_____

Tell me about an adventure you had. Your strangest experience? Your funniest?

_____

_____

_____

_____

Is there a family story, a prayer, an anecdote or saying you would like to have us remember always? What is it? Can you say it in another language?

_____

_____

_____

_____

_____

What second chances did you get in life, and did they work out for you?

_____

_____

_____

_____

What are the strengths that get you through the hard times?

_____

_____

_____

_____

What are the wisest things you know?

_____

_____

_____

_____

_____

What is your own personal golden rule?

_____

_____

_____

_____

Do you have a recipe for happiness that you can share with me?

_____

_____

_____

_____

Were you ever foolish? In what way?

_____

_____

_____

_____

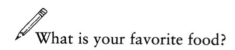 What was a defining moment in your life?

_____

_____

_____

_____

What were your fears in growing up, and were you able to overcome them? Is there something you can tell me to help me in my own life?

_____

_____

_____

_____

What is your favorite food?

_____

_____

_____

_____

What do you hold sacred in life?

_____

_____

_____

_____

_____

Did you ever forgive someone for a hurt done to you?

_____

_____

_____

_____

_____

What were some of the obstacles you have overcome in your life?

_____

_____

_____

_____

_____

What is the most courageous thing you ever did? The most foolhardy?

_____

_____

_____

_____

What is the biggest risk you ever took, and how did it work out?

_____

_____

_____

_____

What do you feel passionate about?

_____

_____

_____

_____

Did you ever have a pet you loved with all your heart?

_____

_____

_____

_____

What was your favorite movie? Song? Poem? Saying?

_____

_____

_____

_____

What questions in life would you like to see answered?

_____

_____

_____

_____

If you could perform a miracle, what would it be?

_____

_____

_____

_____

_____

Who are the people most special to you?

_____

_____

_____

_____

_____

If you could redo one thing in your life, what would it be, and how would you do it?

_____

_____

_____

_____

If you could go back to one moment in time, when would that be?

_____

_____

_____

_____

_____

What have you learned from the young people in your life?

_____

_____

_____

_____

_____

What is the meaning of life?

_____

_____

_____

_____

_____

What makes for a successful human being?

_____

_____

_____

_____

If you could take a long walk with anyone in your family, past or present, who would it be, and why? What would you say to them?

_____

_____

_____

_____

If there were no tomorrow, what would you do today?

_____

_____

_____

_____

If you could create something beautiful for the world, what would it be?

_____

_____

_____

_____

What will be the next milestone in your life?

_____

_____

_____

_____

What is your religion? Were you raised in a particular religious faith or belief? Do you believe in God?

_____

_____

_____

_____

_____

Looking ahead, what things do you want to accomplish in life? What are your dreams?

_____

_____

_____

_____

If you had your life to do all over again, what would you do differently?

_____

_____

_____

_____

Are there any thoughts you'd like to add?

_____

_____

_____

_____

_____

Thank you for sharing these memories with me. I have learned much from you.

CHAPTER SIX

My Questions and Notes

Here is space for you to note additional questions that you would like to ask or that have arisen while you were doing the interviews. Jot down any thoughts or impressions that come to mind, as well as any explanatory family information you want to remember. Date them, too.

For example, you might want to write down expressions used in the tapes that are in another language and translate them.

You can also use this space as a journal to write about the feelings that came flooding to you from the interviews. They are worth capturing.

_____

_____

_____

_____

_____

_____

_____

_____

_____

_____

_____

_____

_____

_____

_____

_____

_____

_____

"Make Beliefs" Activities to Do Together

One of the ways you can learn more about the person you are interviewing for an instant oral biography is to sit down with them, pencils, pens or crayons in hand, and write, draw or color your responses to the "Make Beliefs" illustrated features that follow.

Not only will this activity draw you closer to each other, but these completed pages will provide you both with much fun and knowledge as you turn to your imagination for answers. Date them and include the names of the people who completed the "Make Beliefs." This visual feature can accompany your taped or written interviews. Enjoy!

WOULD YOU GO WITH YOUR LIFE?

IMAGÍNESE
QUE TUVIERA ALAS PARA VOLAR,
¿ A DÓNDE IRÍA CON
SU VIDA?

DATE

You Can Write, Draw and Color Here

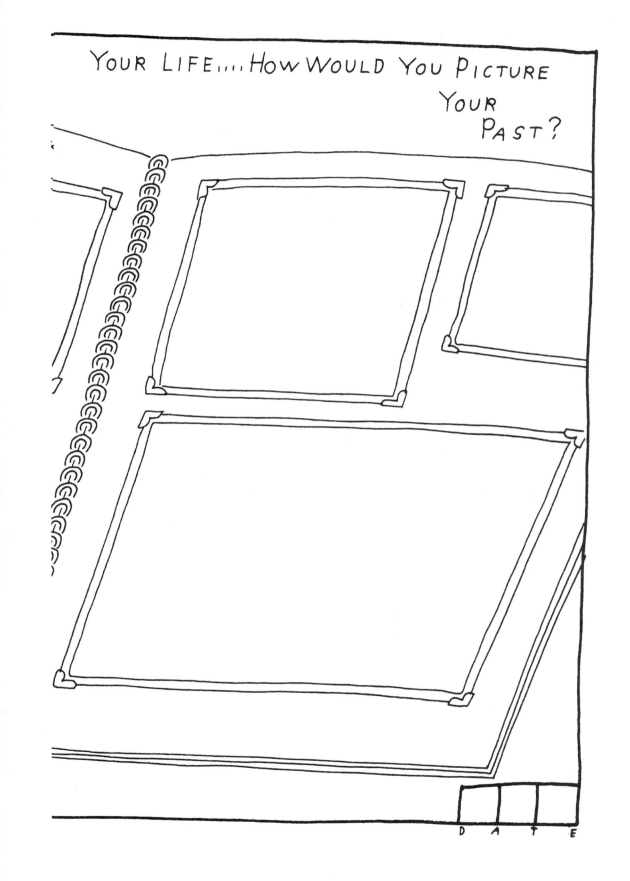

YOUR LIFE....HOW WOULD YOU PICTURE YOUR PAST?

DATE

You Can Write, Draw And Color Here

MAKE BELIEVE YOU COULD PLAY AGAIN WITH AN OLD, OLD FRIEND

WHO WOULD YOU PICK TO PLAY WITH?

WHAT WOULD YOU PLAY?

DATE

You Can Write, Draw And Color Here

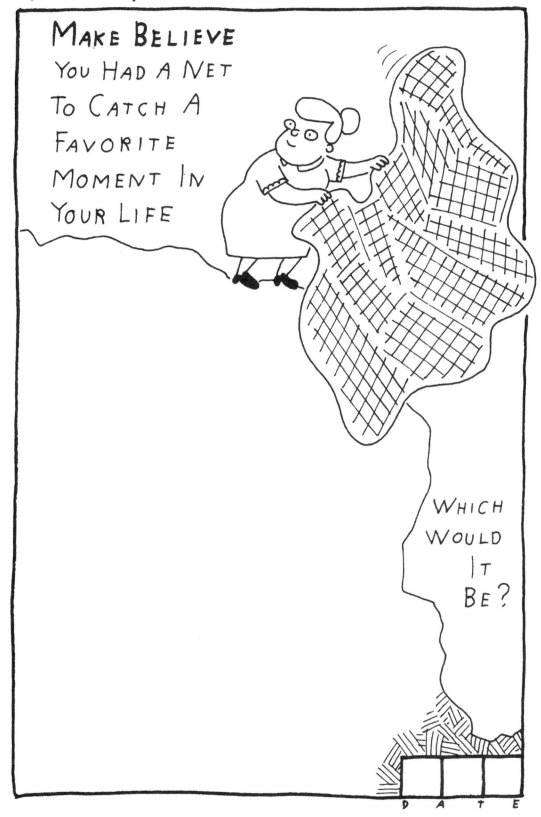

MAKE BELIEVE
YOU CREATED
YOUR OWN
SWEET BLESSING
FOR
SOMEONE
YOU
LOVE

WHAT WOULD IT BE ?

DATE

Family Time Capsules To Complete for the New Millennium

J ust think! In taping your instant oral biographies of the people who are dear to you, you are helping the generations that will be born in the New Millennium. Your audiotapes, videotapes or written notes, which safeguard the memories of people who lived in the twentieth century, will provide valuable information that will guide family members who will be living in the twenty-first century and beyond.

The memories you record provide a "time capsule" of another time and place. But the hopes and dreams and predictions that people have for the new century also can be placed into this time capsule. On the pages that follow you will find many questions aimed at eliciting the future expectations of your relatives or friends.

After the people you interview record their responses to these "time capsules" questions about the future, you can place these sacred responses in a safe, dry place, such as a steel or plastic "treasure chest" file marked "To Be Opened in the Twenty-first Century" (say, around the year 2050). When storing these predictions, you can place photographs of the people who make them, as well as mementos they might want to be discovered by a future generation, along with them: a favorite CD or poem, for example.

In completing the time capsules that follow, don't forget to jot down the name of the person making the prediction, their family relationship, and the date, including the year it was made. Don't be compulsive: Choose to answer only those time capsules that appeal to you and the person you are interviewing. This task of thinking about the future should not be seen as a burden; rather, it is simply a fun way of tapping into a person's imagination to gain a more complete look at their view of life and their hopes for things to come. While no one really knows what the future will hold, each of us is still capable of using our imaginations to become an "instant" seer.

Some day, some very lucky person will hear, see or read these completed time capsules predictions, and they'll smile or laugh or be amazed at how an ancestor viewed the future. What a wonderful gift to posterity.

Time Capsules

A repository to safekeep your thoughts for future discovery. (Fill in and save for the New Millennium. Date them and sign your name.)

These are the things that I hope will go on forever and ever in our world, no matter what change lies ahead:

_____

_____

_____

These are some of the things I plan to do to make the world a better place for the future:

_____

_____

Here's my prediction for a key scientific or medical discovery to be made in the twenty-first century:

_____

_____

Here's my greatest hope for the new century:

_____

_____

Here's a question for someone living in the year 2099 that I'd love to see answered:

_____

_____

Here's my biggest fear about the future:

_____

_____

This is what I think the hit television show, movie or book will be in the year 2050 (if possible, give name and premise):

_____

_____

_____

Here's how I think we'll be entertained in the New Millennium:

_____

_____

Here's how we'll spend our weekends in the year 2050:

_____

_____

This is my prediction about war and peace:

_____

_____

These are the kinds of new jobs people will be doing by the middle of the century:

_____

_____

These are the ten things I would place in a time capsule today to give someone opening it in the year 2099 a good sense of what life was like today—particularly the important things. (Don't worry about limitations—you have access to the entire Library of Congress, to film and TV archives, to anything you want—just think about what truly is important to place in the time capsule.):

1. _____

2. _____

3. _____

4. _____

5. _____

6. _____

7. _____

8. _____

9. _____

10. _____

Here's how I think the family unit will evolve over the next 1,000 years:

_____

_____

This is what I think life will be like 100 years from today:

_____

_____

These are the beliefs and values that I think will be as true 1,000 years from now as they are today:

_____

_____

_____

This is the message I would hope our government will heed in the year 2099:

_____

_____

The biggest change I foresee for us is:

_____

_____

This is the challenge I would like to see the world meet over the next 100 years:

_____

_____

How do you want to be known to future generations?

_____

_____

What blessing would you give to me and our family to protect us for the New Millennium?

_____

_____

What principle should guide our family in the years to come?

_____

_____

What advice can you offer us for the New Millennium?

_____

_____

What challenge would you throw out to our family to meet for the New Millennium?

_____

_____

In the new century, what do you hope to accomplish?

_____

_____

What prayer is uppermost in your heart as you greet the New Millennium?

_____

_____

If you were writing the scenario for a science fiction story or movie for the year 2099, what would it be about?

_____

_____

_____

What has been the most important event in your own lifetime?

_____

_____

How will our world be transformed over the next 25, 50, 100, 500 or even 1,000 years?

_____

_____

Make believe you could ride a time machine into the future, or even back into the past. Where would you want it to take you?

_____

_____

What problems do you think will still be around 75 years from now? Which ones will we have been able to solve by then?

_____

_____

If you were planning an expedition around the world to celebrate the New Millennium, what are some of the places that would be on your intinerary? (Yes, you can include other planets, too.)

_____

_____

_____

This is what I think we will have discovered about our universe by the year 2065:

_____

_____

What great new invention do you foresee being created in the next 50 years? What breakthrough?

_____

_____

_____

Here are some quick-and-dirty predictions for the future on

Families: _____

Schools: _____

Health: _____

Environment: _____

Transportation and travel: _____

Work: _____

Entertainment: _____

Human relationships: _____

_____

_____

_____

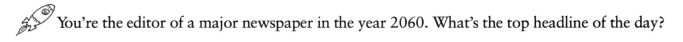 You're the editor of a major newspaper in the year 2060. What's the top headline of the day?

_____

_____

These are some of my designs for fashions that will be worn in the year 2098:

_____

_____

_____

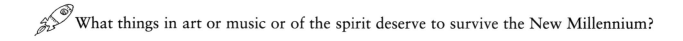 What things in art or music or of the spirit deserve to survive the New Millennium?

_____

_____

What pressing problem in society would you hope to see solved over the next century?

_____

_____

Here's a menu of the foods that I predict we'll be eating in the year 2025:

_____

_____

_____

Here's what we'll be packing in our suitcase 25 years from now:

_____

_____

Here are some subjects that kids will be discussing in school 25 years from now:

_____

_____

_____

You're filling a page in your diary in the year 2025. What will your day be like?

_____

_____

_____

Here's what a young person will be doing on a Friday night in the year 2025:

_____

_____

Create a poem for the New Millennium:

_____

_____

_____

_____

Here's my wildest, craziest prediction for the new century:

_____

_____

_____

If you could have changed some important event in history over the past 1,000 years, what would that have been, and how would you have changed it?

CHAPTER NINE

_____

_____

_____

_____

Rounding Out the Oral Biography

Once you have asked most of the questions you want to ask of a particular person, such as your father or mother or respected friend, interview other relatives or close family friends for their reminiscences about the person you interviewed. This can help give you a fuller picture of the person, for we are seen differently by different people.

In doing this, I suggest you tape another introduction stating whom you are interviewing, the date, what their relationship is to the person they are talking about and whether they bear any relationship to you. Also have them state how long they have know the other person.

In interviewing these family friends or other relatives, you might ask, for example:

- How and when did you meet my (mother, father, aunt, uncle, etc.)?
- What are your recollections of how my (mother, father) was when you first knew (her, him)?

- Has (she, he) changed much in (her, his) ways from when you first knew (her, him)?
- What were some of the adventures you shared together?
- What were your happiest experiences together? Your saddest?
- What is the funniest story you remember about my (mother, father)?
- What do you think are my (mother's, father's) outstanding characteristics?
- What did you learn from her or him?

By the way, this process of gathering other people's impressions of someone can be used to good advantage in trying to capture a spoken portrait of someone who has just died. The tapes help us to remember.

The main goal you are trying to achieve in interviewing friends and relatives is to get their impressions of another person. It would be good to encourage them to give examples and anecdotes.

CHAPTER TEN

Other Uses for Instant Oral Biographies

In making your *Instant Oral Biography* tape library, you also can add tape selections for the purpose of preserving important family and religious traditions. Here are examples:

- How does your family prepare for and celebrate special holidays, such as Christmas, Easter, Three Kings Day, Ramadan, Passover, Chanukah, your favorite holiday? What special foods do we eat? What traditions do we follow?
- What is your recipe to prepare that wonderful (pudding, cake, name dish) you make for Thanksgiving or Christmas? How do you prepare (ham hocks, other dishes)?
- What ceremonies should we observe upon the birth of a boy child? A girl child? Twins?
- What is the proper way to observe periods of mourning? What are our customs during and after a burial and the annual observance of a death?
- What other rituals or customs do we follow for special occasions, such as birthdays, observing religious holidays, a period of engagement or the exchange of marriage vows?

- What are your favorite family sayings? Who started them? Is there a way to say them in the language that was originally spoken in our family?
- What are some of the home remedies our family has handed down from generation to generation to treat certain ailments, such as a bad cold, upset stomach or rashes?
- Tell me about some family superstitions. Or what things can I do to make my dreams come true or have good luck?
- Are there any family diseases we suffer from, and what are the symptoms we should watch for?
- Are there special toasts we say in our family?
- What are some good planting hints?
- Are there other family traditions you would like us to keep alive? What are they?

Instant Biographies Help Archive Changes

The tapes can also provide us with a way to compile living records of each new generation's development.

For example, I have used the tape recorder to great advantage to make tapes of my daughter's first words and the stories she has told us. Interview your own children.

In interviewing my daughter, I want to know what makes her happy, sad or frightened. I want to understand her view of life, what she considers to be her best joke or most difficult riddle, her favorite (or most hated) person. What kinds of people does she like? What are some of her goals? What dreams does she remember? What nightmares? What wishes does she have? What advice can she offer me so that I can remember to enjoy life as openly as she? "Sing a song for me that you love," I ask her. "Read to me the story you wrote."

Today, a young woman, Carlota enjoys listening to how she spoke or sang at younger age. We have also used the recorder to tape some of her favorite stories, which she can play when she is on trips away from home.

You might want to use the recorder to tape special events or ceremonies, such as the exchange of marriage vows, a Passover seder, a Bar or Bat Mitzvah, a religious service, a family prayer or an important speech.

Use the interview technique to understand more clearly your own feelings and those of other people.

Those who are hospitalized for illness might consider taping their own feelings and experiences during treatment and recovery to help others who may go through the same sickness. These can be donated to a lending library at medical treatment centers.

Many communities, through their local libraries, historical societies or religious institutions, are using the oral history approach to compile a historical picture of their communities by interviewing local leaders and residents who have been around for some time.

Similarly, corporations can use this same approach to interview their senior executives, who can trace the development of their enterprises over the years.

For children from divorced families where remarriages have occurred, or children who are adopted, the oral biographies approach provides a way for them to learn and draw closer to their new relatives. And for newlyweds, taping interviews with new family members provides a rich way to learn about each other's backgrounds. Why not exchange tapes with your vows and your hopes for the future together?

And for those about to go abroad to live or travel, why not consider taping oral biographies of family members who are close to you so that you can hear their voices when you are far away?

Interview yourself with the tape recorder to capture your impressions of what you see or learn during your exterior or interior journeys: What impresses you? What frightens you? What strikes you as funny? What do you feel?

The "Mechanical Diary"

The tape recorder thus becomes a mechanical diary by which you hold onto and understand your thoughts and feelings. Sometimes, mail someone close to you such a cassette as you would a letter.

Remember, the approach you take to compiling *Instant Oral Biographies* should reflect your own interests and emphasize the type of information you personally want to preserve for generations to come, as well as for yourself.

I hope you enjoy the process. I believe it can provide you with a wonderful way of finding your story and preserving the best parts of your life.

CHAPTER ELEVEN

What Is a Family? Questions for the Changing Family

I smiled, and almost cried, when I recently saw the cover of a major national news weekly showing one of our country's most powerful newspaper executives, a white man, with his wife, a person of Hispanic origin, and their four adopted children—one blond and blue eyed, the other three of mixed race and color. The cover story about multiracial families told of the efforts by four families who chose to adopt children of races other than their own and how they were making their lives together.

Much of the world has changed as far as families and relationships are concerned since the time 20 years ago when I first wrote this book. We have learned that families are not created in only one way or follow the same model.

At the time I sat down to write this book, I was struggling to find a way to reconcile with my family, which had originally rejected my wife because she came from a different racial, cultural and religious background than mine. I so wanted my family to accept her and love our birth daughter, who was a blend of all that was good in each of us. This was a time, you must remember, when there were not so many

interracial, interreligious marriages and families as there are today, when people often could not clearly see the person beneath the different skin color.

The Changing Family

But since that time, families and relationships have become as diverse and rich as the imagination allows. In addition to multiracial, multicultural families, there are those headed by single parents, both men and women, straight as well as gay. These families may include children who were adopted, born of surrogate parents, or conceived by artificial insemination and in vitro fertilization. There are families headed by parents who have been divorced and who have had more than one spouse, with each partner often bringing children from previous marriages to create a new family. There are families made up of foster children. There are families where children are being raised by grandparents or relatives rather than by birth parents. There are transracial families where children wear different hues from the parents. There are extended families, too, sometimes with older generations living with younger ones. Sometimes, within one household, there may be a number of adults sharing the responsibility of raising the young people born there. Or perhaps you are one of those who have created a new family made up of loved friends.

We are learning that a family is whatever unit that can effectively provide love and nurturing to a child and the group's members. All this change, which can be confusing at times, still makes our lives all the richer, and means that in tracing family history, there are more things to be discovered and more to learn than ever before. There are new stories to be learned and questions to be asked.

For such families doing their oral biographies, most of the questions posed in the "Questions to Ask" chapter of this book will do the job. But for such special families, some additional questions may be useful to include in your interviews.

For those who are members of multicultural marriages, an interviewer might want to ask:

- Tell me about the richness of the different sides of our family. What are the heritages we share? Where was I born?
- Please tell me some of the stories that capture who we are as a people. What makes us distinct and special?
- Did you face discrimination when you and mother (or dad) first married? Did your family and society accept your coming together? How has the world changed since you came together?
- If we come from different cultures and races, then what am I?
- What religion do you observe? What religion should I observe?
- What future would you like to see for me?

For children of adoptive parents:

- Tell me your earliest memory of me. What was I like? Why and how did you choose me to be your child? Was it a hard process for you to adopt me? Where was I born?
- What do you know about my birth mother and father? Who were they? What were they like? Why did they give me up?
- What was your life like before I came into it? How has my joining you changed your life?
- What are your hopes and expectations for me?
- What are the struggles of being an adopting parent?

For children of divorced parents who also may have a stepparent or stepsibling:

- Why did you and mother (father) break up?
- What is your earliest memory of me?
- Tell me about the different sides of our birth family and our stepfamily. Where do we come from?
- How hard is it to be a stepparent—what are the difficult parts? The easy parts?
- How do you define a family?
- What future would you like to see for me?

For children of gay parents:

- What was it like to be gay when you were growing up?
- How did you discover you were gay? How did it make you feel, and how did society and your family treat you?
- What was your life like before you had me? How did you choose me? Where was I born?
- How has my coming changed your life?
- What will I be like when I grow up? Will I be gay or not?

- When you got together with your partner, was the world a welcoming or hostile place to you? What discrimination have you faced in your life? And how did you get through it?
- What are the struggles and rewards of being a gay parent?
- How do you define a family?
- What are your hopes and dreams for us?

Just as traditional family structures are changing, so, too, must family trees. In outlining our family trees, we need to find ways to accommodate the growing diversity in families—some being created through domestic or international adoptions, children of gay parents and those born through new reproductive technology, families separated by divorce and then rebuilt with stepparents and stepsiblings, as well as children raised by relatives or foster parents.

On the following page is a new kind of family tree orchard that has several kinds of trees you can fill in.

One includes birth parents and relatives. Another includes adoptive parents and relatives. And yet another includes those loving, nurturing people—such as friends and godparents—who, while not related to us by birth, are very, very dear to us and whom we often regard as our "real" family. You may want to include them in your family tree outline.

In the trees on that page, list those people who are important to your life, state their relationship to you and the years of their life. You are free to add more trees or branches to meet your needs.

I am sure there are other family situations that I have not outlined here. But I think, from reading these questions, you get the point. Never be wed just to the questions posed in this book; always be ready to add your own to make your instant oral biographies richer and more meaningful to your own life. Your basic goal is to learn about other human beings and, in turn, to learn about yourself.

Use the blank family tree below to fill in the names of the people important in your life. On the signpost, explain who is in your family tree. You can label it **My Birth Family** or **My Adoptive Family** or **The Nuturing People in My Life**—whatever you want.

Name

Relationship

Name

Relationship

Name

Relationship

Name

Relationship

Name

Relationship

Name

Relationship

Name

Relationship

Name

Relationship

Name

Relationship

Name

Relationship

Name

Relationship

Name

Relationship

Name

Relationship

Name

Relationship

Name

Relationship

Name

Relationship

CHAPTER TWELVE

Family History Sheets

The family history sheets that follow are not meant to be definitive; rather, they are designed to help you delineate your family relationships in some organized form.

Each of the tables has been duplicated in order to allow each partner in a relationship to use it for outlining his or her own family organizations. Feel free to modify them to suit your particular needs.

Part 1: One Side of the Family

FOR A FAVORITE PHOTO

MY FAMILY

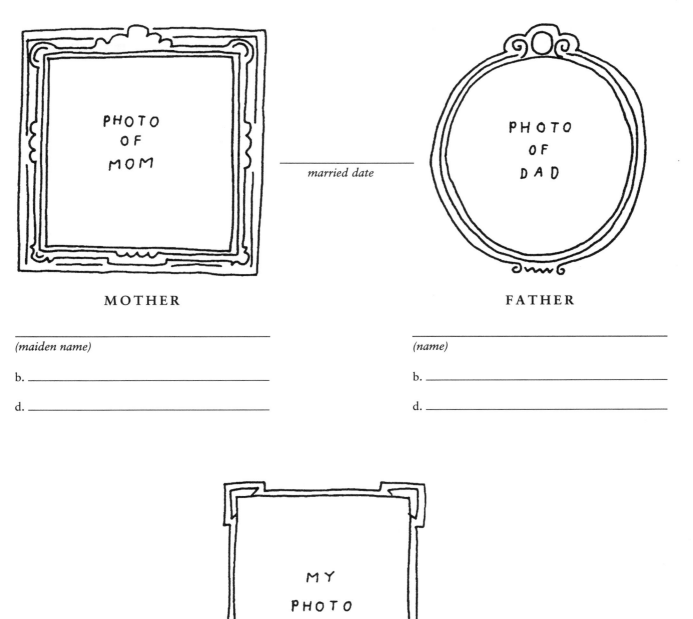

MOTHER

_____

(maiden name)

b. _____

d. _____

FATHER

_____

(name)

b. _____

d. _____

ME

_____

(my name)

b. _____

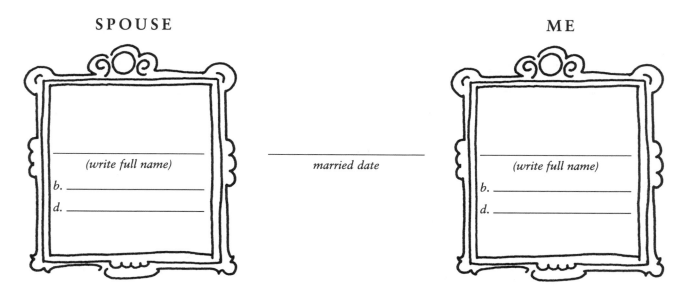

SPOUSE

ME

(write full name)

b. _____

d. _____

married date

(write full name)

b. _____

d. _____

My Children and Grandchildren

First Born _____

  b. _____ d. _____

  Marriage date _____

  Spouse _____

  b. _____ d. _____

  Children:

  1. _____

  b. _____ d. _____

  2. _____

  b. _____ d. _____

Second Born _____

  b. _____ d. _____

  Marriage date _____

  Spouse _____

  b. _____ d. _____

  Children:

  1. _____

  b. _____ d. _____

2. _____

b. _____ d. _____

Third Born _____

b. _____ d. _____

Marriage date _____

Spouse _____

b. _____ d. _____

Children:

1. _____

b. _____ d. _____

2. _____

b. _____ d. _____

Other personal or historical data that you may want to note. You can include educational accomplishments, trades and professions, other important dates, burial sites, remarriages or places of birth:

_____

_____

_____

_____

_____

_____

_____

_____

_____

_____

_____

_____

_____

_____

_____

My Other Marriages:

To whom _____

    b. _____ d. _____

    Marriage years _____

Children of marriage:

    First born _____

    b. _____ d. _____

    Child's marriage date _____

    Child's spouse _____

    b. _____ d. _____

    First born's children:

    1. _____

    b. _____ d. _____

    2. _____

    b. _____ d. _____

    Second born _____

    b. _____ d. _____

    Child's marriage date _____

    Child's spouse _____

    b. _____ d. _____

    Second born's children:

    1. _____

    b. _____ d. _____

2. _____

b. _____ d. _____

Other personal or historical data:

_____

_____

_____

_____

_____

_____

_____

_____

_____

Spouse's Other Marriages:

To whom _____

b. _____ d. _____

Marriage years _____

Children of marriage:

First born _____

b. _____ d. _____

Child's marriage date _____

Child's spouse _____

b. _____ d. _____

First born's children:

1. _____

b. _____ d. _____

2. _____

b. _____ d. _____

Second born _____

b. _____ d. _____

Child's marriage date _____

Child's spouse _____

b. _____ d. _____

Second born's children:

1. _____

b. _____ d. _____

2. _____

b. _____ d. _____

Other personal or historical data:

_____

_____

_____

_____

_____

_____

_____

_____

_____

_____

_____

_____

_____

_____

_____

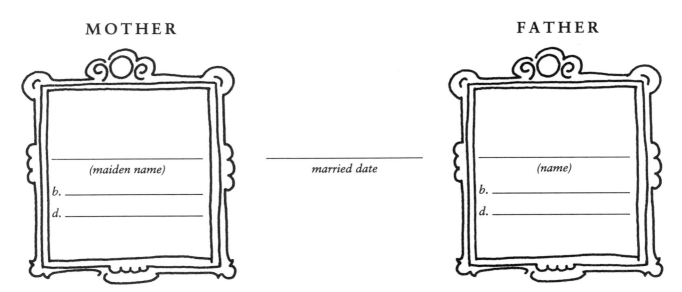

MOTHER   FATHER

(maiden name)

b. _____

d. _____

married date

(name)

b. _____

d. _____

Me, My Brothers and Sisters

First Born _____

 b. _____ d. _____

 Marriage date _____

 Spouse _____

 b. _____ d. _____

 Children:

 1. _____

 b. _____ d. _____

 2. _____

 b. _____ d. _____

Second Born _____

 b. _____ d. _____

 Marriage date _____

 Spouse _____

 b. _____ d. _____

 Children:

 1. _____

 b. _____ d. _____

2. _____

b. _____ d. _____

Third Born _____

b. _____ d. _____

Marriage date _____

Spouse _____

b. _____ d. _____

Children:

1. _____

b. _____ d. _____

2. _____

b. _____ d. _____

Fourth Born _____

b. _____ d. _____

Marriage date _____

Spouse _____

b. _____ d. _____

Children:

1. _____

b. _____ d. _____

2. _____

b. _____ d. _____

Other personal or historical data:

_____

_____

_____

_____

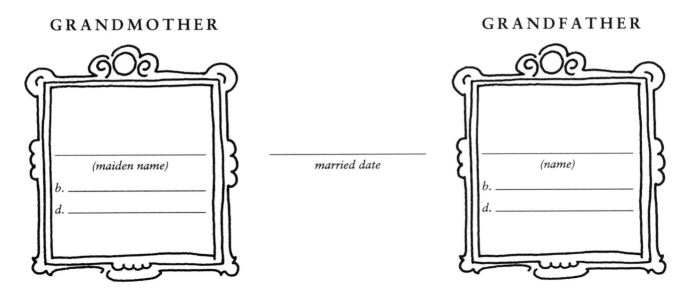

GRANDMOTHER

(maiden name)

b. _____

d. _____

married date

GRANDFATHER

(name)

b. _____

d. _____

My Mother, Her Brothers and Sisters

First Born _____

b. _____ d. _____

Marriage date _____

Spouse _____

b. _____ d. _____

Children:

1. _____

b. _____ d. _____

2. _____

b. _____ d. _____

Second Born _____

b. _____ d. _____

Marriage date _____

Spouse _____

b. _____ d. _____

Children:

1. _____

b. _____ d. _____

2. _____

b. _____   d. _____

Third Born _____

b. _____   d. _____

Marriage date _____

Spouse _____

b. _____   d. _____

Children:

1. _____

b. _____   d. _____

2. _____

b. _____   d. _____

Fourth Born _____

b. _____   d. _____

Marriage date _____

Spouse _____

b. _____   d. _____

Children:

1. _____

b. _____   d. _____

2. _____

b. _____   d. _____

Other personal or historical data:

_____

_____

_____

_____

GRANDMOTHER   GRANDFATHER

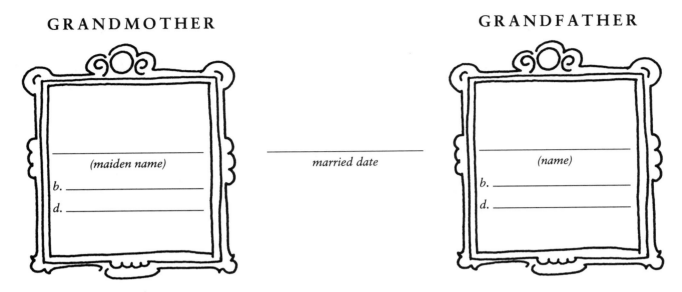

(maiden name)   married date   (name)

b. _____   b. _____

d. _____   d. _____

My Father, His Brothers and Sisters

First Born _____

   b. _____ d. _____

   Marriage date _____

   Spouse _____

   b. _____ d. _____

   Children:

   1. _____

   b. _____ d. _____

   2. _____

   b. _____ d. _____

Second Born _____

   b. _____ d. _____

   Marriage date _____

   Spouse _____

   b. _____ d. _____

   Children:

   1. _____

   b. _____ d. _____

2. _____

b. _____ d. _____

Third Born _____

b. _____ d. _____

Marriage date _____

Spouse _____

b. _____ d. _____

Children:

1. _____

b. _____ d. _____

2. _____

b. _____ d. _____

Fourth Born _____

b. _____ d. _____

Marriage date _____

Spouse _____

b. _____ d. _____

Children:

1. _____

b. _____ d. _____

2. _____

b. _____ d. _____

Other personal or historical data:

_____

_____

_____

_____

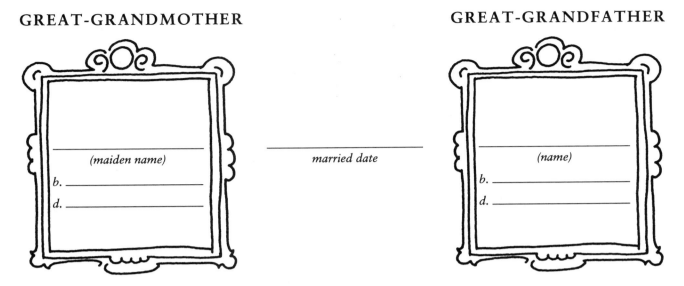

GREAT-GRANDMOTHER

_____ (maiden name)
b. _____
d. _____

married date

GREAT-GRANDFATHER

_____ (name)
b. _____
d. _____

My Maternal Grandmother, Her Brothers and Sisters

First Born _____

b. _____ d. _____

Marriage date _____

Spouse _____

b. _____ d. _____

Children:

1. _____
b. _____ d. _____

2. _____
b. _____ d. _____

Second Born _____

b. _____ d. _____

Marriage date _____

Spouse _____

b. _____ d. _____

Children:

1. _____
b. _____ d. _____

2. _____

b. _____ d. _____

Third Born _____

b. _____ d. _____

Marriage date _____

Spouse _____

b. _____ d. _____

Children:

1. _____

b. _____ d. _____

2. _____

b. _____ d. _____

Fourth Born _____

b. _____ d. _____

Marriage date _____

Spouse _____

b. _____ d. _____

Children:

1. _____

b. _____ d. _____

2. _____

b. _____ d. _____

Other personal or historical data:

_____

_____

_____

_____

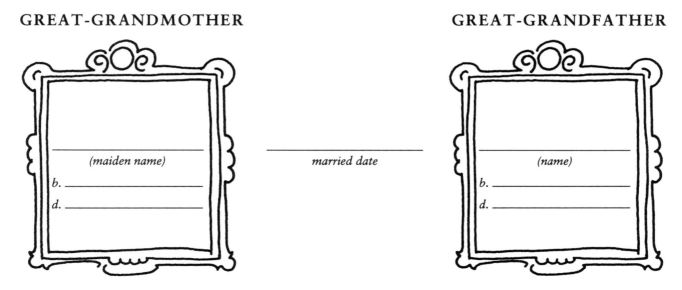

GREAT-GRANDMOTHER

_____
(maiden name)
b. _____
d. _____

_____
married date

GREAT-GRANDFATHER

_____
(name)
b. _____
d. _____

My Maternal Grandfather, His Brothers and Sisters

First Born _____

   b. _____ d. _____

   Marriage date _____

   Spouse _____

   b. _____ d. _____

   Children:

    1. _____

    b. _____ d. _____

    2. _____

    b. _____ d. _____

Second Born _____

   b. _____ d. _____

   Marriage date _____

   Spouse _____

   b. _____ d. _____

   Children:

    1. _____

    b. _____ d. _____

2. _____

   b. _____ d. _____

Third Born _____

   b. _____ d. _____

Marriage date _____

Spouse _____

   b. _____ d. _____

Children:

   1. _____

   b. _____ d. _____

   2. _____

   b. _____ d. _____

Fourth Born _____

   b. _____ d. _____

Marriage date _____

Spouse _____

   b. _____ d. _____

Children:

   1. _____

   b. _____ d. _____

   2. _____

   b. _____ d. _____

Other personal or historical data:

_____

_____

_____

_____

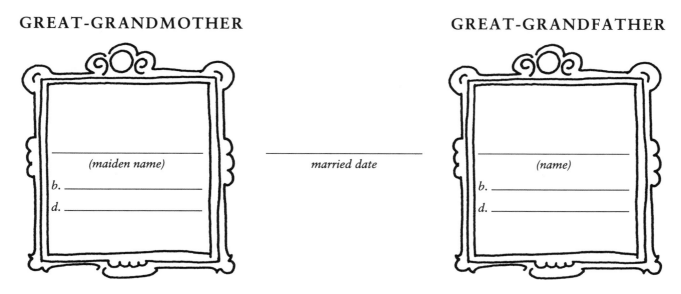

GREAT-GRANDMOTHER

GREAT-GRANDFATHER

_____ (maiden name)

b. _____

d. _____

_____ married date

_____ (name)

b. _____

d. _____

My Paternal Grandmother, Her Brothers and Sisters

First Born _____

  b. _____ d. _____

  Marriage date _____

  Spouse _____

  b. _____ d. _____

  Children:

  1. _____

  b. _____ d. _____

  2. _____

  b. _____ d. _____

Second Born _____

  b. _____ d. _____

  Marriage date _____

  Spouse _____

  b. _____ d. _____

  Children:

  1. _____

  b. _____ d. _____

2. _____

b. _____ d. _____

Third Born _____

b. _____ d. _____

Marriage date _____

Spouse _____

b. _____ d. _____

Children:

1. _____

b. _____ d. _____

2. _____

b. _____ d. _____

Fourth Born _____

b. _____ d. _____

Marriage date _____

Spouse _____

b. _____ d. _____

Children:

1. _____

b. _____ d. _____

2. _____

b. _____ d. _____

Other personal or historical data:

_____

_____

_____

_____

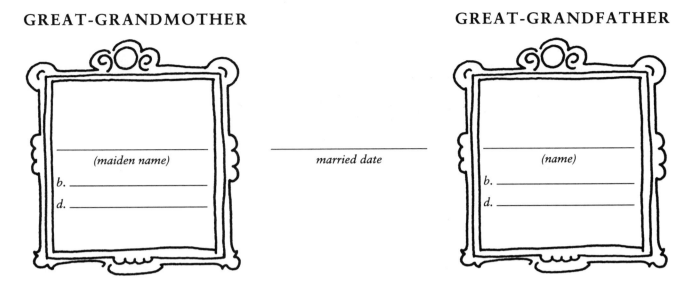

GREAT-GRANDMOTHER

_____
(maiden name)

b. _____

d. _____

GREAT-GRANDFATHER

_____
(name)

b. _____

d. _____

_____
married date

My Paternal Grandfather, His Brothers and Sisters

First Born _____

b. _____ d. _____

Marriage date _____

Spouse _____

b. _____ d. _____

Children:

1. _____

b. _____ d. _____

2. _____

b. _____ d. _____

Second Born _____

b. _____ d. _____

Marriage date _____

Spouse _____

b. _____ d. _____

Children:

1. _____

b. _____ d. _____

2. _____

b. _____ d. _____

Third Born _____

b. _____ d. _____

Marriage date _____

Spouse _____

b. _____ d. _____

Children:

1. _____

b. _____ d. _____

2. _____

b. _____ d. _____

Fourth Born _____

b. _____ d. _____

Marriage date _____

Spouse _____

b. _____ d. _____

Children:

1. _____

b. _____ d. _____

2. _____

b. _____ d. _____

Other personal or historical data:

_____

_____

_____

_____

Part Two: The Other Side of the Family

_____

(Family's Name)

SPOUSE

(maiden name)

b. _____

d. _____

_____
married date

ME

(name)

b. _____

d. _____

My Children and Grandchildren

First Born _____

    b. _____ d. _____

    Marriage date _____

    Spouse _____

    b. _____ d. _____

    Children:

    1. _____

    b. _____ d. _____

    2. _____

    b. _____ d. _____

Second Born _____

    b. _____ d. _____

    Marriage date _____

    Spouse _____

    b. _____ d. _____

    Children:

    1. _____

    b. _____ d. _____

    2. _____

    b. _____ d. _____

Third Born _____

    b. _____ d. _____

    Marriage date _____

    Spouse _____

    b. _____ d. _____

    Children:

    1. _____

b. _____ d. _____

2. _____

b. _____ d. _____

Other personal or historical data that you may want to note. You can include educational accomplishments, trades and professions, other important dates, burial sites, remarriages or places of birth:

_____

_____

_____

_____

_____

_____

_____

_____

_____

_____

_____

_____

_____

_____

_____

My Other Marriages:
To whom _____

b. _____ d. _____

Children of marriage:

First born _____

b. _____ d. _____

Child's marriage date _____

Child's spouse _____

b. _____ d. _____

First born's children:

1. _____

b. _____ d. _____

2. _____

b. _____ d. _____

Second born _____

b. _____ d. _____

Child's marriage date _____

Child's spouse _____

b. _____ d. _____

Second born's children:

1. _____

b. _____ d. _____

2. _____

b. _____ d. _____

Other personal or historical data:

_____

_____

_____

_____

_____

_____

_____

Spouse's Other Marriages:

To whom _____

    b. _____ d. _____

    Marriage years _____

Children of marriage:

    First born _____

    b. _____ d. _____

    Child's marriage date _____

    Child's spouse _____

    b. _____ d. _____

    First born's children:

    1. _____

    b. _____ d. _____

    2. _____

    b. _____ d. _____

    Second born _____

    b. _____ d. _____

    Child's marriage date _____

    Child's spouse _____

    b. _____ d. _____

    Second born's children:

    1. _____

    b. _____ d. _____

    2. _____

    b. _____ d. _____

Other personal or historical data:

_____

_____

_____

_____

_____

_____

_____

_____

_____

_____

_____

_____

_____

_____

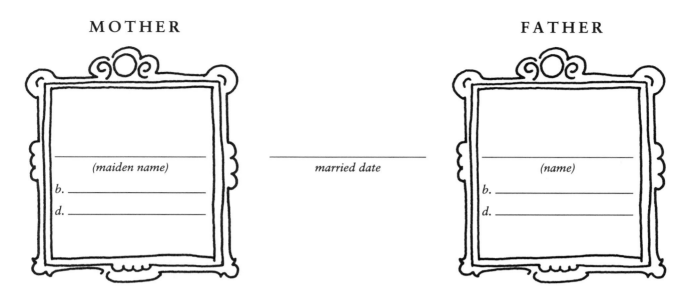

MOTHER   FATHER

_____   _____
(maiden name)   (name)
b. _____   b. _____
d. _____   d. _____

_____
married date

Me, My Brothers and Sisters

First Born _____

b. _____ d. _____

Marriage date _____

Spouse _____

b. _____ d. _____

Children:

1. _____

b. _____ d. _____

2. _____

b. _____ d. _____

Second Born _____

b. _____ d. _____

Marriage date _____

Spouse _____

b. _____ d. _____

Children:

1. _____

b. _____ d. _____

2. _____

b. _____ d. _____

Third Born _____

b. _____ d. _____

Marriage date _____

Spouse _____

b. _____ d. _____

Children:

1. _____

b. _____ d. _____

2. _____

b. _____ d. _____

Fourth Born _____

b. _____ d. _____

Marriage date _____

Spouse _____

b. _____ d. _____

Children:

1. _____

b. _____ d. _____

2. _____

b. _____ d. _____

Other personal or historical data:

_____

_____

_____

_____

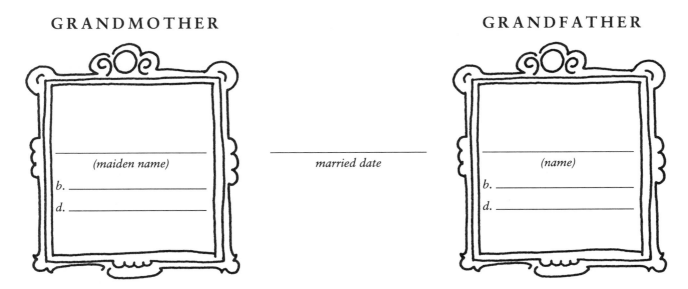

GRANDMOTHER GRANDFATHER

_____
(maiden name)

married date

_____
(name)

b. _____
d. _____

b. _____
d. _____

My Mother, Her Brothers and Sisters

First Born _____

b. _____ d. _____

Marriage date _____

Spouse _____

b. _____ d. _____

Children:

1. _____

b. _____ d. _____

2. _____

b. _____ d. _____

Second Born _____

b. _____ d. _____

Marriage date _____

Spouse _____

b. _____ d. _____

Children:

1. _____

b. _____ d. _____

2. _____

b. _____ d. _____

Third Born _____

b. _____ d. _____

Marriage date _____

Spouse _____

b. _____ d. _____

Children:

1. _____

b. _____ d. _____

2. _____

b. _____ d. _____

Fourth Born _____

b. _____ d. _____

Marriage date _____

Spouse _____

b. _____ d. _____

Children:

1. _____

b. _____ d. _____

2. _____

b. _____ d. _____

Other personal or historical data:

_____

_____

_____

_____

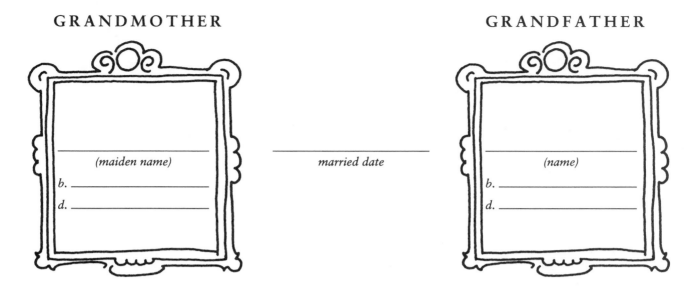

GRANDMOTHER   GRANDFATHER

_____   _____
(maiden name)   married date   (name)

b. _____   b. _____
d. _____   d. _____

My Father, His Brothers and Sisters

First Born _____

    b. _____ d. _____

    Marriage date _____

    Spouse _____

    b. _____ d. _____

    Children:

    1. _____

    b. _____ d. _____

    2. _____

    b. _____ d. _____

Second Born _____

    b. _____ d. _____

    Marriage date _____

    Spouse _____

    b. _____ d. _____

    Children:

    1. _____

    b. _____ d. _____

2. _____

b. _____ d. _____

Third Born _____

b. _____ d. _____

Marriage date _____

Spouse _____

b. _____ d. _____

Children:

1. _____

b. _____ d. _____

2. _____

b. _____ d. _____

Fourth Born _____

b. _____ d. _____

Marriage date _____

Spouse _____

b. _____ d. _____

Children:

1. _____

b. _____ d. _____

2. _____

b. _____ d. _____

Other personal or historical data:

_____

_____

_____

_____

GREAT-GRANDMOTHER   GREAT-GRANDFATHER

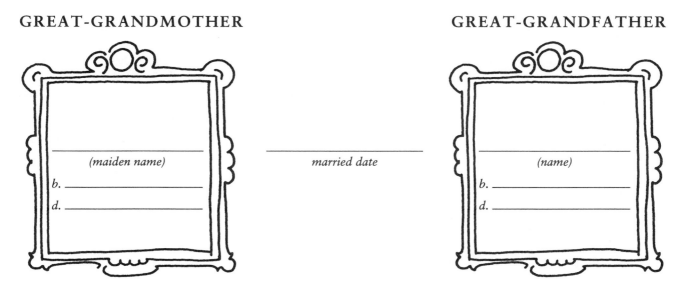

_____ (maiden name)

_____ married date

_____ (name)

b. _____

d. _____

b. _____

d. _____

My Maternal Grandmother, Her Brothers and Sisters

First Born _____

    b. _____ d. _____

    Marriage date _____

    Spouse _____

    b. _____ d. _____

    Children:

    1. _____

    b. _____ d. _____

    2. _____

    b. _____ d. _____

Second Born _____

    b. _____ d. _____

    Marriage date _____

    Spouse _____

    b. _____ d. _____

    Children:

    1. _____

    b. _____ d. _____

2. _____

b. _____ d. _____

Third Born _____

b. _____ d. _____

Marriage date _____

Spouse _____

b. _____ d. _____

Children:

1. _____

b. _____ d. _____

2. _____

b. _____ d. _____

Fourth Born _____

b. _____ d. _____

Marriage date _____

Spouse _____

b. _____ d. _____

Children:

1. _____

b. _____ d. _____

2. _____

b. _____ d. _____

Other personal or historical data:

_____

_____

_____

_____

GREAT-GRANDMOTHER

_____
(maiden name)
b. _____
d. _____

_____
married date

GREAT-GRANDFATHER

_____
(name)
b. _____
d. _____

My Maternal Grandfather, His Brothers and Sisters

First Born _____

    b. _____ d. _____

    Marriage date _____

    Spouse _____

    b. _____ d. _____

    Children:

    1. _____

    b. _____ d. _____

    2. _____

    b. _____ d. _____

Second Born _____

    b. _____ d. _____

    Marriage date _____

    Spouse _____

    b. _____ d. _____

    Children:

    1. _____

    b. _____ d. _____

2. _____

    b. _____ d. _____

Third Born _____

    b. _____ d. _____

Marriage date _____

Spouse _____

    b. _____ d. _____

Children:

    1. _____

    b. _____ d. _____

    2. _____

    b. _____ d. _____

Fourth Born _____

    b. _____ d. _____

Marriage date _____

Spouse _____

    b. _____ d. _____

Children:

    1. _____

    b. _____ d. _____

    2. _____

    b. _____ d. _____

Other personal or historical data:

_____

_____

_____

_____

GREAT-GRANDMOTHER

GREAT-GRANDFATHER

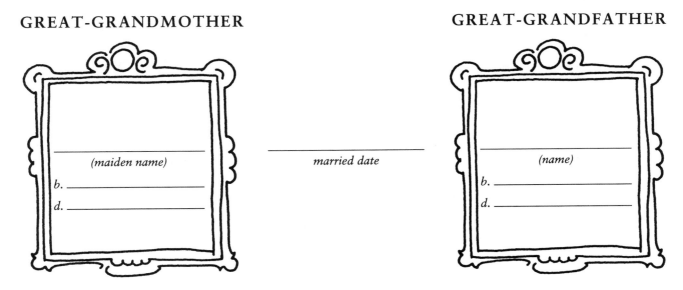

(maiden name)

b. _____

d. _____

married date

(name)

b. _____

d. _____

My Paternal Grandmother, Her Brothers and Sisters

First Born _____

    b. _____ d. _____

    Marriage date _____

    Spouse _____

    b. _____ d. _____

    Children:

    1. _____

    b. _____ d. _____

    2. _____

    b. _____ d. _____

Second Born _____

    b. _____ d. _____

    Marriage date _____

    Spouse _____

    b. _____ d. _____

    Children:

    1. _____

    b. _____ d. _____

2. _____

b. _____ d. _____

Third Born _____

b. _____ d. _____

Marriage date _____

Spouse _____

b. _____ d. _____

Children:

1. _____

b. _____ d. _____

2. _____

b. _____ d. _____

Fourth Born _____

b. _____ d. _____

Marriage date _____

Spouse _____

b. _____ d. _____

Children:

1. _____

b. _____ d. _____

2. _____

b. _____ d. _____

Other personal or historical data:

_____

_____

_____

_____

GREAT-GRANDMOTHER

GREAT-GRANDFATHER

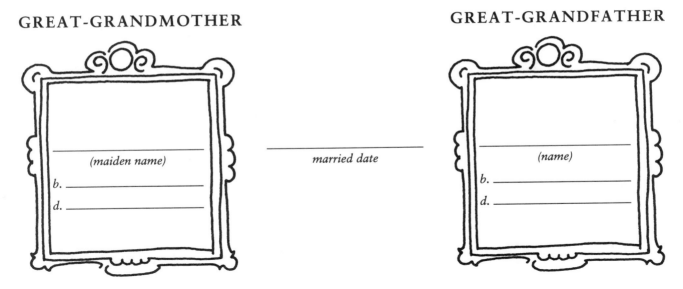

(maiden name)

b. _____

d. _____

_____ married date _____

(name)

b. _____

d. _____

My Paternal Grandfather, His Brothers and Sisters

First Born _____

    b. _____ d. _____

    Marriage date _____

    Spouse _____

    b. _____ d. _____

    Children:

    1. _____

    b. _____ d. _____

    2. _____

    b. _____ d. _____

Second Born _____

    b. _____ d. _____

    Marriage date _____

    Spouse _____

    b. _____ d. _____

    Children:

    1. _____

    b. _____ d. _____

2. _____

   b. _____ d. _____

Third Born _____

   b. _____ d. _____

Marriage date _____

Spouse _____

   b. _____ d. _____

Children:

   1. _____

   b. _____ d. _____

   2. _____

   b. _____ d. _____

Fourth Born _____

   b. _____ d. _____

Marriage date _____

Spouse _____

   b. _____ d. _____

Children:

   1. _____

   b. _____ d. _____

   2. _____

   b. _____ d. _____

Other personal or historical data:

CHAPTER THIRTEEN

_____

_____

_____

_____

A Personal Essay: What I Learned From My Own Family

I first got the idea for writing this book 20 years ago while vacationing with my wife and daughter on the island of Martha's Vineyard, off the coast of Massachusetts.

Taking my young daughter to the local library to borrow some taped story cassettes to play on her recorder, I discovered some unmarked cassettes in an old dusty box. When played that evening, the tapes revealed themselves to be interviews, made by young children, of elderly nursing home residents who had lived on the island for 80 to 90 years. The stories the older people told the children were wonderful—there was richness to be gained from elders sharing their lives with the young.

And as a newspaper editor who had taught many young people how to be journalists, I decided to write a book to teach anyone with the interest how to become a family journalist.

But it was only many years after I wrote this book that I really began to understand why I had written this *particular* book, which brings family members closer together by encouraging them to talk with, and learn from, one another. This bringing together of generations was something I wanted very badly at that time

in my life as a young father who was more clearly beginning to link the past and the future.

The interviews I undertook with my own mother to test the ideas in this book provided a way for me to draw closer to her after a long period of estrangement. Years earlier she had given my wife, Teodorina, and me much pain when she rejected my wife because she was of a different ethnic, racial and religious background than my own. In the early years of my marriage, my mother could not look beyond the brown skin of my Puerto Rican wife to see her as another human being.

Reuniting Loved Ones

I think now that in writing this book, and later by interviewing my mother for her life story, I was desperately searching for a way to reunite my family. I was trying to make peace with my mother and to repair some of the rupture that had occurred in our lives.

I had other motivations, too. Coming from a divorced home, I wanted to learn more about my father, who died when I was only a boy, and to understand better why my parents had such difficulties in living together. I thought, too, that capturing my family's stories and memories on tape would be a wonderful way to preserve some of my family history for my own daughter, Carlota, then six. I wanted her to know more about the backgrounds of her grandparents. She accompanied me when I interviewed my mother, chiming in with her own questions which, ultimately, helped bring her closer to her grandmother.

Doing an oral biography of my mother proved to be a wonderful experience. While they did not entirely console my pain, the many hours spent questioning and listening to my mother and piecing together her oral biography did bring us closer together—and even helped my wife, and me, understand my mother better.

I learned some wonderful stories about my family, and play the tapes from time to time, gaining something different each time, for as I mature I bring to the listening of the tapes the wider perspective that comes with time and understanding.

Learning About the Past

I learned, for example, how my great grandmother, a peddler of elastic and sundries from her pushcart on New York City's lower east side, would have her grandchildren stretch the elastic in order to wring out a few more cents of profit on the goods.

I learned how, at the beginning of their marriage, after coming to this country from Europe early in this century, my maternal grandparents would perform song-and-dance skits for the family on Saturday evenings to cheer their children and themselves when times were hard.

I learned how my mother had to leave school to get a job to help support her large family.

I learned, too, about the dream of my father, a furrier, to become a gentleman farmer some day.

I heard how my parents met in a subway and fell in love, and how my father pursued my mother until she consented to become his wife.

I listened quietly as my mother told me she was sorry for the harsh way she had treated my wife after our marriage. She was happy, my mother said, that Teodorina and I had made a good life together and had given her a granddaughter. She told me that we were doing a good job in raising our child, something I, as an unsure father, needed to hear.

Later, my wife, our daughter and I sat down with my mother-in-law, Pastora, to record her life history, too.

She told us how she had come many years earlier to New York by ship from Puerto Rico to join her sister and make a new life on the mainland. Lovingly, she described the farm where she was born and raised, and how she would ride a horse and hide from her mother in the orange groves. Sitting high on her horse, she could pick oranges from the trees. She told us how hard she and the other children were worked by her grandparents to help the farm, and the family survive.

And so, slowly, tape by tape, my daughter learned about the richness of her background—the Russian, Polish Jewish side of her father's family and the Hispanic, African and Indian side of her mother's.

Since that time, I have conducted oral biographies interviews with many other people, not only family members. These interviews have helped me better understand that human experience, no matter what one's background, is universal. I've learned that each of us shares many of the same joys, fears, hopes and dreams, that no matter how different we may look from one another, underneath, where our souls reside, we are also very much alike.

It's comforting for each of us to learn we are not the only ones who have ever experienced problems in life, and that others have done so too and survived. Sometimes the way they solved their problems has pointed the way for me, too. Each of us, I learned from the oral biographies, holds the spirit and strength to endure. Preparing such oral biographies has helped me feel less alone in the world and more linked to others. I hope they do that for you, too.

—B.Z.

Bill Zimmerman and his daughter, Carlota, interview Pastora Arena Garcia, grandmother. Looking at old photos sparks memories.

Learning by Asking: A Guide for Educators

For some time now I have been encouraging and helping educators teach young people how to become family or neighborhood journalists and interview their close relatives and friends.

The tape recorder enables us to capture these stories on tape and create new kinds of home, school or classroom reference libraries of spoken history, or *Instant Oral Biographies*. We can go there and play cassettes to help us answer the questions we have about life the same way we play tapes of music. Videotape recorders, if available, can be used, too.

Educators and parents find having young people interview others for their life stories is an excellent way to learn about history, social studies, cultural differences and journalism. The answers and new perspectives gained from interviewing people of different backgrounds help all of us little by little fill in the mosaic of what it means to live in this world.

Moreover, conducting an interview certainly enhances language, listening and memory skills, and helps instill self-confidence in young people, particularly shy ones or those with speech problems. It provides a structure that propels them to reach out to another person.

Let us also not minimize the value of interviews as tools to awaken empathy and sensitivity to others, and appreciation of good journalistic skills.

Children Sharing Their Family Histories

I encourage schools to use oral history interviews as focal points for "Grandparents' Day" activities in which relatives, foster parents or close family friends are invited to school to spend time with the children and be questioned about their experiences.

The children take turns in interviewing as well as in "sharing" the relatives and friends who come, since there are never enough around. Similar activities linking the generations can be held at senior citizen centers and hospital nursing homes.

Some nursing homes, in fact, have begun programs involving local schools and colleges and volunteers to help their residents overcome their estrangement from the community at large. They are aware that older people are a prime source for firsthand historical knowledge about their communities, and students who interview these people can preserve important pieces of local history that otherwise would be lost to future generations.

There is an African saying to the effect that when an old person dies, an entire library is destroyed. We must remember this.

Creating Family History Teaching Units

Creative teachers can build exciting teaching units around taping such interviews.

For example, for history, if a class is studying the subject of immigration, class visitors could be asked why and how they came to this country, what life was like for them at first, and how this country differed from their country of birth.

The children, too, might be encouraged to draw family trees as an introduction to genealogical research.

If a class is studying another important historic period, such as the Great Depression, visitors could be asked for firsthand information about how they survived this harsh time and how their lives changed.

A teacher creating a social studies unit about cultural differences could encourage students to interview relatives to tape recipes for special foods cooked during holidays, or ask about customs associated with these special holidays.

For civics, the *Instant Oral Biography* interviewing techniques also can be used to encourage children to visit people in the community, to ask them about their jobs or how the town or neighborhood has changed during the years.

Research teams can be assigned to certain projects—one to interview people who work in government, another to interview entrepreneurs, one to interview scientists and another to question artists.

The children could ask these people how they chose their professions, what they like or dislike about them, how they prepared for them and how they keep developing.

Or, how about an assignment called "Lessons From Life," where children interview adults about what it's like to be a parent, or what grownups were like when they were the children's age, what they were afraid of at that age, what they did to overcome a big problem or what special things they learned that they are proud of.

We learn from such tapes that people of all backgrounds often share similar fears and feelings; in other instances we find people approach the same problems in different ways because of their own individual and cultural differences.

We also find that there usually is no simple answer to an interviewer's question, that more often than not shades of gray predominate over black or white. And that we each have pieces of the full answer.

This is particularly evident when a child interviews two people in the same family and each gives a different version of the same story or incident—but from their special perspective. This is a journalist's first lesson.

Oral Biographies as Reference Material

Completed tapes become new reference tools. Some schools, in fact, are using them to initiate oral history libraries where children can come to play a tape of someone's life for reference or for pleasure in the same way they come to borrow a book.

Teachers also might want to encourage youngsters to take notes while interviewing, even though a tape recorder is being used. Not only does such note-taking prove useful if a recorder fails, but note-taking often helps us listen more carefully and reinforces certain points made.

I would encourage children to form their own questions so that any interview is more meaningful to what they are interested in. These questions can be written on cards, with the specific questions selected for a child on the basis of his or her ability to reach and articulate them.

Sample Questions

Questions can, of course, be selected by the children from those listed in this book. I have found from working with very young people that they are most interested in asking older people for stories about the way they were when they were the children's age. For that reason, here are some very basic questions that could be used for a class taping:

- What is your full name? Do you know what your name means? In what language?
- When were you born? Where were you born?
- When did your family first come to this country, and where did they come from? Did they ever tell you what life was like for them before they came here? What did they bring with them?
- What are your earliest memories of when you were a child? Did you have a nickname?
- What was your life like when you were my age? What did you do with your time when

you were very young—go to school or work? Where did you live? What games did you play?
- Can you tell me any stories to show me the way you were when you were very young?
- What do you think is the most important thing that ever happened to you in your life? What was your greatest adventure?
- Do you remember any especially funny or sad stories about your life?
- What special things do you know that you are proud of?
- Are there favorite family stories, sayings or songs that you can tell me? Can you tell them in a different language? Can you translate them for me? Are there superstitions in your family?
- What things do you enjoy doing the most?
- What advice can you offer me?

These are just sample questions; the best ones would be those made up by the children themselves and which reflect what they want to learn from their elders.

It would be good to tell the youngsters that the answers they get will often raise even more questions about a subject, and that they should feel free enough to follow up on a question before starting a new subject. Thinking quickly and improvising new questions to reflect the turn of a conversation are things that all good journalists do. It is important that children be encouraged to listen carefully to the conversation and follow its course, rather than just going through the interview by rote, ticking off one prepared question after another.

Class visitors should be asked to bring family documents, scrapbooks, passbooks, birth certificates, naturalization and marriage papers, old photographs and maps to show where they came from or once lived. They also can be encouraged to wear the native dress of those countries where they were born, or to bring handcrafts from these places. Maybe even special foods can be prepared for this special day. Children and adults together can also fill in the "Make Beliefs" activity pages in Chapter 7 of this book.

And if you know in advance which relatives are coming, why not have the children research the countries of origin, their history and culture, so that they can ask more informed questions?

Before a class taping is held, have the children practice asking the questions, whether by interviewing each other or their parents at home. In this way they are more comfortable when the actual interviewing takes place.

Also, it has been my experience that when a number of grandparents come to school, it is best to ask each to work with a group of four to six children; this allows every youngster to ask at least a question or two. Also, conduct the interviews one at a time so that other children in the class benefit from hearing the stories and observing the interview process. One interview at a time also helps keep the sound level down in a class; it makes for poor taping and concentration to have many interviews conducted simultaneously.

Youngsters also should be encouraged to write or phone requests for interviews and offer follow-up thank-yous.

And, to reinforce what the children have learned and to improve reading, writing and editing skills, teachers also might want to consider encouraging youngsters to transcribe the

tapes and bind the pages in book form.

We always learn something new in hearing or reading a story for a second time. Again, while making the tape or after rehearing it, you could have the interviewers write a summary sheet of the subjects covered and where on the tape they are found. (Use the counter on the recorder for this.) How about including a glossary of unfamiliar expressions or words in another language?

These transcriptions can also provide the raw material for writing scripts for radio or video programs that a class might want to present to the rest of the school or to parents.

As for obtaining enough recording equipment to go around the class, it has been my experience from organizing such projects that many parents are only too glad to lend tape recorders to a class when they are informed by note of what a teacher is trying to accomplish.

Encourage the parents to have the children practice interviewing with them and help their children gather old family photographs or documents that could be used in the oral biographies.

And how about inviting the school or local newspaper to cover this important event?

Educators also might encourage children to interview each other and share experiences. For example, the interviews might be focused on a theme such as: My Strangest Experience; How I Can Become More Powerful; If I Had Three Wishes; The Things I Know Best; My Saddest Memory; The Happiest Day in My Life; My Biggest Fear and How I Try to Overcome It.

And to help stimulate creativity, why not consider having the children answer questions in a language they make up by themselves and write an accompanying dictionary to help others understand what they are saying.

Finally, for language teachers, the interviews also provide good practice for those trying to speak or understand another language. For practice you might want to ask the questions in the language of the person you interview, with that person answering you in your own language. Such interviews also help prepare a child who has difficulties with language to communicate more effectively for real-life experiences, such as applying for a job or to school. Interviewing is a perfect activity for speech therapy, too.

One of the greatest benefits derived from encouraging individuals to become interviewers is that they are drawn closer to other people just by the process of having to interact with someone through a question-and-answer format. They gain confidence, too.

This process can be undertaken not only by normal children, but also by exceptional ones who may be blind or learning impaired, and who suffer from other physical and emotional handicaps.

Teachers and parents can modify the oral biography interview procedures for the particular needs of such children. This may mean, for example, having a youngster ask only one question of someone in order to ensure that he or she can make the achievement of obtaining an appropriate answer or story. Being able to ask a question, obtain an answer and hear both on tape can go a long way to enhance a child's self-image.

Children with special needs know what it is to face and overcome rejection by others who fear or do not understand them. But, with the interaction that comes from good interviewing, not only can these youngsters learn to communicate more effectively with others, but they can also overcome in part other people's fear of their differences.

Good interviewing helps to enhance the self-image of all people—normal and exceptional.

Please Offer Us Some Free Advice

Dear Reader,

I'd like very much to hear from you and learn from your experiences in using *How to Tape Instant Oral Biographies*. By sending me your suggestions and ideas, you will be helping me improve the content of this book to help future readers.

I'd like, for example, to learn some of the questions or interviewing techniques you used that help provoke interesting responses from the people you interviewed. I'd love to hear some of the wonderful stories you learned about your family, or the family sayings or superstitions you picked your during your tapings. What surprising things did you learn?

Or, what free advice did your older relatives give you in showing you how to live a fuller, more happy life? I'd like to hear what people told you about how they got through the tough times in their lives—how they moved the clouds to let the sunshine in—and what "life lines," or sayings of hope, they used to comfort themselves during hard times. We can all benefit from hearing these.

And if you give your written permission (including your name and address), I might try to use some of your words in other books I write. For every suggestion that I use in my books, I will send you one of my books. A gift for a gift.

So please help me make *How to Tape Instant Oral Biographies* a more useful, living book.

Please write to:
Bill Zimmerman
c/o Guarionex Press
201 W. Seventy-Seventh St.
New York, NY 10024

Thank you and happy taping!

Bill Zimmerman

Bill Zimmerman

Other Books By Bill Zimmerman:

A Book of Questions

Make Beliefs: A Gift Book for Your Imagination

Lifelines: A Book of Hope

The Little Book of Joy

Dogmas: Simple Truths From a Wise Pet

Make Beliefs for Kids of All Ages

A Book of Sunshine

Cat-e-Chisms: Feline Answers to Life's Big Questions

ABOUT THE AUTHOR

Bill Zimmerman, the creator of *How to Tape Instant Oral Biographies*, has been a questioner all his life.

A journalist for more than twenty-five years, Zimmerman is special projects editor of *Newsday*, one of the nation's largest daily newspapers, and creator/editor of its nationally syndicated Student Briefing Page on the News. His page was nominated by *Newsday* for a Pulitzer Prize.

His other books are: *Make Beliefs*, a book for the imagination that readers can complete with pencil, crayon or paintbrush; *Dogmas: Simple Truths From a Wise Pet*; *Cat-e-Chisms: Feline Answers to Life's Big Questions*; *Make Beliefs for Kids of All Ages*; *The Little Book of Joy*, an interactive book of prayers and meditations; *A Book of Questions*, a new form of diary/journal; *Lifelines: A Book of Hope*, which offers comforting thoughts to help people get through difficult times in life; and *A Book of Sunshine*, which moves the clouds in your life.

Zimmerman originally published *Instant Oral Biographies* under the imprint of his kitchen-table press, Guarionex Press, as a way to better understand his own family.

As a child, he loved to listen to family stories, and truly believes everyone has a story to tell.

Tom Bloom, who illustrated this book, dreams and draws for *The New York Times*, *The New Yorker*, *Newsday*, *The Wall Street Journal* and other publications. He has illustrated many books and lives in New York with his family.

INDEX